INTRODUCTION TO
BUDDHISM

HOPE THESE WORDS OF WISDOM GETS YOU
TO WHERE YOU WANT TO GO; ON
A PEACEFUL PATH. I WOULD LIKE
TO TELL YOU THAT I FEEL VERY
FORTUNATE TO HAVE MET YOU, AND
I HOPE OUR FRIENDSHIP CAN BE
A VERY BEAUTIFUL ONE.

LOVE ALWAYS,
ROB.

Also by Geshe Kelsang Gyatso

Cover illustration The lotus flower is a traditional Buddhist symbol of purity. A lotus is born from the mud at the bottom of a lake but blossoms above the water as a stainless flower that brings pleasure to all who behold it. In a similar fashion, living beings are born in the ocean of suffering with impure bodies and impure minds; but if they train in meditation they can attain a completely pure body and mind, and bring peace and happiness to all who meet them.

INTRODUCTION TO
BUDDHISM

AN EXPLANATION OF THE
BUDDHIST WAY OF LIFE

Geshe Kelsang Gyatso

Tharpa Publications
London

First published in 1992
Revised edition 1993

Tharpa Publications
15 Bendemeer Road
London SW15 1JX

Cover design by Losang Wangchuk
Cover illustration by Robert Beer
Cover photo of Geshe Kelsang Gyatso by Gerry Hale
Line illustrations by Andy Weber

British Library Cataloguing in Publication Data
A catalogue record for this book is available
from the British Library.

ISBN 0 948006 26 9 – papercase
ISBN 0 948006 27 7 – paperback

Set in Palatino by Tharpa Publications
Printed on acid-free longlife paper and bound
in Great Britain by Redwood Books, Trowbridge, Wiltshire

Contents

Illustrations

Acknowledgements

This book, *Introduction to Buddhism*, is an exceptionally clear explanation of the Buddhist way of life. From the depths of our hearts we thank the author, Venerable Geshe Kelsang Gyatso, for his immeasurable kindness in preparing this book, which provides a definitive introduction to Buddhism for those in the West.

The author was assisted in the initial stages of editing by Michael Garside. The full draft was passed on to Gen Thubten Gyatso (Neil Elliott) for final editing, and checked closely by the author. It was then prepared for publication by Lucy James, Sherab Gyatso, and others in the Tharpa Editorial Office. Our thanks go to all of these dedicated students of the author for their excellent work.

Roy Tyson, Director
Manjushri Mahayana
Buddhist Centre
October 1992

Editorial Note

In recent years there has been a considerable growth of interest in Buddhism and in its application to our western way of life. The publication of *Introduction to Buddhism* therefore is both timely and welcomed.

The author, Geshe Kelsang Gyatso, who was born in Tibet, is a highly-accomplished Lama, who has been resident in England since 1977. From his studies and meditation in Tibet and India he has developed a profound insight into the teachings of Buddha and a deep and practical experience of their meaning; and from his years spent in England he has developed a thorough understanding of our western way of life. He is therefore ideally placed to write a book introducing Buddhism to the western reader.

If you are not already familiar with the life and teachings of Buddha you may find some of the concepts and practices introduced in this book a little unusual to begin with. However, if you think about them patiently and sincerely you will discover that they are very meaningful and have great relevance to our daily lives. Although Buddhism is an ancient religion that first appeared in the East, the practices taught by Buddha are timeless and universally applicable. These days many people are discovering that Buddhism has answers to questions and solutions to problems that cannot be found elsewhere. It is hoped, therefore, that the publication of this book will help to improve the understanding and deepen the appreciation of Buddhism in the West.

PART ONE

Basic Buddhism

Buddha Shakyamuni

Who was Buddha?

In general, 'Buddha' means 'Awakened One', someone who has awakened from the sleep of ignorance and sees things as they really are. A Buddha is a person who is completely free from all faults and mental obstructions. There are many people who have become Buddhas in the past, and many people will become Buddhas in the future.

The Buddha who is the founder of the Buddhist religion is called Buddha Shakyamuni. 'Shakya' is the name of the royal family into which he was born, and 'Muni' means 'Able One'. Buddha Shakyamuni was born as a royal prince in 624 BC in a place called Lumbini, which was originally in northern India but is now part of Nepal. His mother's name was Queen Mayadevi and his father's name was King Shuddhodana.

One night, Queen Mayadevi dreamed that a white elephant descended from heaven and entered her womb. The white elephant entering her womb indicated that on that very night she had conceived a child who was a pure and powerful being. The elephant's descending from heaven indicated that her child came from Tushita heaven, the Pure Land of Buddha Maitreya. Later, when she gave birth to the child, instead of experiencing pain the queen experienced a special, pure vision in which she stood holding the branch of a tree with her right hand while the gods Brahma and Indra took the child painlessly from her side. They then proceeded to honour the infant by offering him ritual ablutions.

When the king saw the child he felt as if all his wishes had been fulfilled and he named the young prince 'Siddhartha'. He invited a Brahmin seer to make predictions about the prince's future. The seer examined the child with his clairvoyance and told the king 'There are signs that the boy could become either a chakravatin king, a ruler of the entire world, or a fully enlightened Buddha. However, since the time for chakravatin kings is now past it is certain that he will become a Buddha, and that his beneficial influence will pervade the thousand million worlds like the rays of a sun.'

As the young prince grew up, he mastered all the traditional arts and sciences without needing any instruction. He knew sixty-four different languages, each with their own alphabet, and he was also very skilled at mathematics. He once told his father that he could count all the atoms in the world in the time it takes to draw a single breath. Although he did not need to study, he did so to please his father and to benefit others. At his father's request he joined a school where, in addition to studying various academic subjects, he became skilled at sports such as martial arts and archery. The prince would take every opportunity to convey spiritual meanings and to encourage others to follow spiritual paths. At one time, when he was taking part in an archery contest, he declared 'With the bow of meditative concentration I will fire the arrow of wisdom and kill the tiger of ignorance in living beings.' Then he released the arrow and it flew straight through five iron tigers and seven trees before disappearing into the earth! By witnessing demonstrations such as this, thousands of people developed faith in the prince.

Sometimes Prince Siddhartha would go into the capital city of his father's kingdom to see how the people lived. During these visits he came into contact with many old people and sick people, and on one occasion he saw a

4

corpse. These encounters left a deep impression on his mind and led him to realize that all living beings without exception have to experience the sufferings of birth, sickness, ageing, and death. Because he understood the laws of reincarnation he also realized that they experience these sufferings not just once, but again and again, in life after life without cessation. Seeing how all living beings are trapped in this vicious circle of suffering he felt deep compassion for them, and he developed a sincere wish to free all of them from their suffering. Realizing that only a fully enlightened Buddha has the wisdom and the power to help all living beings in this way, he resolved to leave the palace and retire to the solitude of the forest where he would engage in profound meditation until he attained enlightenment.

When the people of the Shakya kingdom realized that the prince intended to leave the palace they requested the king to arrange a marriage for him in the hope that this would cause him to change his mind. The king agreed and soon found him a suitable bride, the daughter of a respected Shakya family, called Yasodhara. Prince Siddhartha, however, had no attachment to worldly pleasures because he realized that objects of attachment are like poisonous flowers, which initially appear to be attractive but eventually give rise to great pain. His resolve to leave the palace and to attain enlightenment remained unchanged, but to fulfil his father's wishes and to bring temporary benefit to the Shakya people, he agreed to marry Yasodhara. However, even though he remained in the palace as a royal prince, he devoted all his time and energy to serving the Shakya people in whatever way he could.

When he was twenty-nine years old the prince had a vision in which all the Buddhas of the ten directions appeared to him and spoke in unison saying 'Previously you resolved to become a Conqueror Buddha so that you could help all living beings trapped in the cycle of suffering. Now is the time for you to accomplish this.' The prince went immediately to his parents and told them of his intention: 'I wish to retire to a peaceful place in the forest where I can engage in deep meditation and quickly attain full enlightenment. Once I have attained enlightenment I will be able to repay the kindness of all living beings, and especially the great kindness that you have shown me. Therefore I request your permission to leave the palace.' When his parents heard this they were shocked and the king refused to grant his permission. Prince Siddhartha said to his father 'Father, if you can give me permanent freedom from the sufferings of birth, sickness, ageing, and death I will stay in the palace; but if you cannot I must leave and make my human life truly meaningful.'

The king tried all means to prevent his son from leaving the palace. In the hope that the prince might change his mind, he surrounded him with a retinue of beautiful women, dancers, singers, and musicians, who day and night used their charms to please him; and in case the prince might attempt a secret escape he posted guards around the palace walls. However, the prince's determination to leave the palace and enter a life of meditation could not be shaken. One night he used his miracle powers to send the guards and attendants into a deep sleep while he made his escape from the palace with the help of a trusted aide. After they had travelled about six miles, the prince dismounted from his horse and bade farewell to his aide. He then cut off his hair and threw it into the sky, where it was caught by the gods of the Land of the Thirty-three Heavens. One of the gods then offered the prince the saffron robes of a religious mendicant. The prince accepted these and gave his royal garments to the god in exchange. In this way he ordained himself as a monk.

Siddhartha then made his way to a place near Bodh Gaya in India, where he found a suitable site for meditation. There he remained, emphasizing a meditation called 'space-like concentration on the Dharmakaya' in which he focused single-pointedly on the ultimate nature of all phenomena. After training in this meditation for six years, he realized that he was very close to attaining full enlightenment and so he walked to Bodh Gaya where, on the full moon day of the fourth month of the lunar calendar, he seated himself beneath the bodhi tree in the meditation posture and vowed not to rise from meditation until he had attained perfect enlightenment. With this determination he entered the space-like concentration on the Dharmakaya.

As dusk fell, Devaputra Mara, the chief of all the demons, or maras, in this world, tried to disturb Siddhartha's concentration by conjuring up many fearful apparitions. He manifested hosts of terrifying demons, some throwing spears, some firing arrows, some trying to burn him with fire, and some hurling boulders and even mountains at him. Siddhartha however remained completely undisturbed. Through the force of his concentration, the weapons, rocks, and mountains appeared to him as a rain of fragrant flowers, and the raging fires became like offerings of rainbow light.

Seeing that Siddhartha could not be frightened into abandoning his meditation, Devaputra Mara tried instead to distract him by manifesting countless beautiful women, but Siddhartha responded by developing even deeper concentration. In this way he triumphed over all the demons of this world, which is why he subsequently became known as a 'Conqueror Buddha'.

Siddhartha then continued with his meditation until dawn, when he attained the vajra-like concentration. With this concentration, which is the very last mind of a limited being, he removed the final veils of ignorance from his mind and in the next moment became a Buddha, a fully enlightened being.

There is nothing that Buddha does not know. Because he has awakened from the sleep of ignorance and has removed all obstructions from his mind, he knows everything of the past, present, and future, simultaneously and directly. Moreover, Buddha has great compassion which is completely impartial, embracing all living beings without discrimination. He benefits all living beings without exception by emanating various forms throughout the universe and by bestowing his blessings on their minds. Through receiving Buddha's blessings, all beings, even the lowliest animals, sometimes develop peaceful and virtuous states of mind. Eventually, through meeting an emanation of Buddha in the form of a Spiritual Guide, everyone will have the opportunity to enter the path to liberation and enlightenment. As the great Indian scholar Nagarjuna said, there is no one who has not received help from Buddha.

Forty-nine days after Buddha had attained enlightenment the gods Brahma and Indra requested him to teach, saying:

O Buddha, Treasure of Compassion,
Living beings are like blind people in constant
    danger of falling into the lower realms.
Other than you there is no Protector in this world.
Therefore we beseech you, please rise from
    meditative equipoise and turn the Wheel of
    Dharma.

As a result of this request, Buddha rose from meditation and taught the first Wheel of Dharma. These teachings, which include the *Sutra of the Four Noble Truths* and other discourses, are the principal source of the Hinayana, or Lesser Vehicle, of Buddhism. Later, Buddha taught the second and third Wheels of Dharma, which include the

Perfection of Wisdom Sutras and the *Sutra Discriminating the Intention* respectively. These teachings are the source of the Mahayana, or Great Vehicle, of Buddhism. In the Hinayana teachings Buddha explains how to attain liberation from suffering for oneself alone, and in the Mahayana teachings he explains how to attain full enlightenment, or Buddhahood, for the sake of others. Both traditions flourished in Asia, at first in India and then gradually in other surrounding countries, including Tibet. Now they are also beginning to flourish in the West.

The reason why Buddha's teachings are called the 'Wheel of Dharma' is as follows. It is said that in ancient times there were great kings, known as chakravatin kings, who used to rule the entire world. These kings had many special possessions, including a precious wheel in which they would travel around the world. Wherever the precious wheel went, the king would control that region. Buddha's teachings are said to be like a precious wheel because wherever they spread, the people in that area have the opportunity to control their minds by putting them into practice.

'Dharma' means 'protection'. By practising Buddha's teachings we protect ourself from suffering and problems. All the problems we experience during daily life originate in ignorance, and the method for eliminating ignorance is to practise Dharma.

Practising Dharma is the supreme method for improving the quality of our human life. The quality of life depends not upon external development or material progress, but upon the inner development of peace and happiness. For example, in the past many Buddhists lived in poor and underdeveloped countries, but they were able to find pure, lasting happiness by practising what Buddha had taught.

If we integrate Buddha's teachings into our daily life we will be able to solve all our inner problems and attain a truly peaceful mind. Without inner peace, outer peace is impossible. If we first establish peace within our minds by training in spiritual paths, outer peace will come naturally; but if we do not, world peace will never be achieved, no matter how many people campaign for it.

Buddhism, or Buddhadharma, is Buddha's teachings and the inner experiences or realizations of these teachings. Buddha gave eighty-four thousand teachings. All these teachings and the inner realizations of them constitute Buddhism. Buddhism can be divided into two parts: basic Buddhism and advanced Buddhism. The essential teachings of basic Buddhism will now be explained in the remainder of Part One of this book, and the more advanced teachings will be introduced in Parts Two and Three.

Understanding the Mind

Buddha taught that everything depends upon the mind. To realize this, we must first understand the nature and functions of the mind. At first this might seem to be quite straightforward since we all have minds, and we all know what state our mind is in – whether it is happy or sad, clear or confused, and so forth. However, if someone were to ask us what the nature of our mind is and how it functions we would probably not be able to give a precise answer. This indicates that we do not have a clear understanding of the mind.

Some people think that the mind is the brain or some other part or function of the body, but this is incorrect. The brain is a physical object that can be seen with the eyes and that can be photographed or operated on in surgery. The mind, on the other hand, is not a physical object. It cannot be seen with the eyes, nor can it be photographed or repaired by surgery. The brain therefore is not the mind but simply part of the body.

There is nothing within the body that can be identified as being our mind because our body and mind are different entities. For example, sometimes when our body is relaxed and immobile our mind can be very busy, darting from one object to another. This indicates that our body and mind are not the same entity. In the Buddhist scriptures our body is compared to a guest house and our mind to a guest dwelling within it. When we die our mind leaves our body and goes to the next life, just like a guest leaving a guest house and going somewhere else.

Buddha Complete Subduer with
the Essence of Vajra

Buddha Jewel of
Radiant Light

Buddha Powerful
King of the Nagas

If the mind is not the brain nor any other part of the body, what is it? It is a formless continuum that functions to perceive and understand objects. Because the mind is formless, or non-physical, by nature, it is not obstructed by physical objects. Thus, it is impossible for our body to go to the moon without travelling in a spaceship, but our mind can reach the moon in an instant just by thinking about it. Knowing and perceiving objects is the uncommon function of the mind. Although we say 'I know such and such', in reality it is our mind that knows. We know things only by using our mind.

There are three levels of mind: gross, subtle, and very subtle. Gross minds include sense awarenesses such as eye awareness and ear awareness, and all strong delusions such as anger, jealousy, attachment, and strong self-grasping ignorance. These gross minds are related to gross inner winds and are relatively easy to recognize. When we fall asleep or die, our gross minds dissolve inwards and our subtle minds become manifest. Subtle minds are related to subtle inner winds and are more difficult to recognize than gross minds. During deep sleep, and at the end of the death process, the inner winds dissolve into the centre of the heart channel wheel inside the central channel, and then the very subtle mind, the mind of clear light, becomes manifest. The very subtle mind is related to the very subtle inner wind and is extremely difficult to recognize. The continuum of the very subtle mind has no beginning and no end. It is this mind that goes from one life to the next, and if it is completely purified by training in meditation it is this mind that will eventually transform into the omniscient mind of a Buddha.

It is very important to be able to distinguish unpeaceful states of mind from peaceful states. States of mind that disturb our inner peace, such as anger, jealousy, and desirous attachment, are called delusions. These are the principal causes of all our suffering. We may think that our suffering is caused by other people, by poor material conditions, or by society, but in reality it all comes from our own deluded states of mind. The essence of Dharma practice is to reduce and eventually to eradicate altogether our delusions and to replace them with peaceful, virtuous states of mind. This is the main purpose of training in meditation.

Normally we seek happiness outside ourself. We try to obtain better material conditions, a better job, higher social status, and so forth; but no matter how successful we are in improving our external situation we still experience many problems and much dissatisfaction. We never experience pure, lasting happiness. In his Dharma teachings Buddha advises us not to seek happiness outside ourself but to establish it within our mind. How can we do this? By purifying and controlling our mind through the sincere practice of Buddhadharma. If we train in this way we can ensure that our mind remains calm and happy all the time. Then, no matter how difficult our external circumstances may be, we will always be happy and peaceful.

Even though we work very hard to find happiness it remains elusive for us, whereas sufferings and problems seem to come naturally, without any effort. Why is this? It is because the cause of happiness within our mind, virtue, is very weak and can give rise to its effect only if we apply great effort, whereas the internal causes of suffering and problems, the delusions, are very strong and can give rise to their effect with no effort on our part. This is the real reason why problems come naturally while happiness is so difficult to find.

From this we can see that the principal causes of both happiness and problems are in the mind, not in the external world. If we were able to maintain a calm and peaceful mind all day long we would never experience any problems or mental suffering. For example, if our mind remains peaceful all the time then even if we are insulted, criticized, or blamed, or if we lose our job or our friends, we will not become unhappy. No matter how difficult our external circumstances may become, for as long as we maintain a calm and peaceful mind the situation will not be a problem for us. Therefore, if we wish to be free from problems there is only one thing to do – to learn to maintain a peaceful state of mind by practising Dharma sincerely and purely.

Buddha Leader of the Heroes

Buddha Glorious Pleasure

Buddha Jewel Fire

Past and Future Lives

If we understand the nature of the mind we can also understand the existence of past and future lives. Many people believe that when the body disintegrates at death the continuum of the mind ceases and the mind becomes non-existent, like a candle flame going out when all the wax has burned. There are even some people who contemplate committing suicide in the hope that if they die their problems and sufferings will come to an end; but these ideas are completely wrong. As already explained, our body and mind are separate entities, and so even though the body disintegrates at death the continuum of the mind remains unbroken. Instead of ceasing, the mind simply leaves the present body and goes to the next life. For ordinary beings, therefore, rather than releasing us from suffering, death only brings new sufferings. Not understanding this, many people destroy their precious human life by committing suicide.

In his Tantric teachings Buddha taught a special practice called 'transference of consciousness into another body'. This practice became quite widespread in the early days of Buddhism in Tibet. One practitioner who mastered it was Tarma Dode, the son of the famous Tibetan lay Lama and translator, Marpa. One day, while riding a horse, Tarma Dode fell and fatally injured his body. Knowing that his son had mastered the practice of transference of consciousness, Marpa immediately began searching for a corpse into which Tarma Dode could transfer his consciousness. Unable to find a human corpse, Marpa brought his son a pigeon's corpse, which would serve as a temporary abode for his mind until he could find a suitable human corpse. Tarma Dode then ejected his mind from his dying human body and entered into the corpse of the pigeon. Immediately, Tarma Dode's old human body died and the pigeon's body came back to life. Tarma Dode's body was now the body of a pigeon, but his mind was still the mind of a human being.

Since he did not want his son to remain in the form of a pigeon, Marpa continued to search for a qualified human corpse. One day, with his clairvoyance, he saw that a Buddhist Teacher had just died in India and that his disciples had taken his corpse to the cemetery. Marpa told his son to fly to India as quickly as possible. Tarma Dode then flew to India in his pigeon's body and, when he arrived at the place where the Teacher's corpse had been left, he ejected his mind from the pigeon's body and entered the corpse. The body of the pigeon immediately died and the body of the deceased Teacher came back to life. Tarma Dode then spent the remainder of his life as an Indian Teacher known as Tiwu Sangnak Dongpo. Some years later, Marpa's principal disciple, Milarepa, sent his own disciple, Rechungpa, to India to receive special teachings from Tiwu Sangnak Dongpo. When Rechungpa returned to Tibet, he offered these instructions to Milarepa.

There are many other examples of past meditators who could transfer their consciousness into other bodies. It is said that Marpa himself practised transference of consciousness into another body four times during his life. If mind and body were the same entity, how would it be possible for these meditators to transfer their consciousness in this way? If we contemplate true stories such as these with a positive mind it will help us to understand how it is possible for consciousness to continue beyond the death of the body. This in turn will make it very easy for us to understand the existence of past and future lives.

Another way in which we can gain an understanding of past and future lives is to examine the process of sleep, dreaming, and waking, because this closely resembles the process of death, intermediate state, and rebirth. When we fall asleep, our gross inner winds gather and dissolve inwards and our mind becomes progressively more and more subtle until it transforms into the very subtle mind of the clear light of sleep. While the clear light of sleep is manifest we experience deep sleep, and to others we resemble a dead person. When it ends, our mind becomes gradually more and more gross and we pass through the various levels of the dream state. Finally, our normal powers of memory and mental control are restored and we wake up. When this happens, our dream world disappears and we perceive the world of the waking state.

A very similar process occurs when we die. As we die, our winds dissolve inwards and our mind becomes progressively more and more subtle until the very subtle mind of the clear light of death becomes manifest. The experience of the clear light of death is very similar to the experience of deep sleep. After the clear light of death has ceased, we experience the stages of the intermediate state, or bardo in Tibetan, which is a dream-like state that occurs between death and rebirth. After a few days or weeks, the intermediate state ends and we take rebirth. Just as when we wake from sleep the dream world disappears and we perceive the world of the waking state, so when we take rebirth the appearances of the intermediate state cease and we perceive the world of our next life.

The only significant difference between the process of sleep, dreaming, and waking and the process of death, intermediate state, and rebirth is that after the clear light of sleep has ceased the relationship between our mind and our present body remains intact, whereas after the clear light of death this relationship is broken. By contemplating this we will gain conviction in the existence of past and future lives.

We generally believe that the things we perceive in dreams are unreal whereas the things we perceive when we are awake are true; but Buddha said that all phenomena are like dreams in that they are mere appearances to mind. For those who can interpret them correctly, dreams have great significance. For example, if we dream that we visit a particular country to which we have not been in this life, our dream will indicate one of four things: that we have been to that country in a previous life, that we will visit it later in this life, that we will visit it in a future life, or that it has some personal significance for us, as it would, for example, if we had recently received a letter from that country or had seen a television programme about it. Similarly, if we dream we are flying, it may mean that in a previous life we were a being who could fly, such as a bird or a meditator with miracle powers, or it may predict that we will become such a being in the future. A flying dream may also have a less literal meaning, symbolizing an improvement in our health or state of mind.

It was with the help of dreams that I was able to discover where my mother was reborn after she had died. Just before she died, my mother dozed off for a few minutes and when she woke she told my sister, who was attending her, that she had dreamed of me and that in her dream I had offered her a traditional white scarf, or *khatag*. I took this dream to mean that I would be able to help my mother in her next life and so, after she died, I prayed every day for her to be reborn in England, where I was living, so that I would have the opportunity to meet and recognize her reincarnation. I made strong requests to my Dharmapala to show me clear signs of where my mother's reincarnation could be found.

Later I had three dreams which seemed to be significant. In the first, I dreamed that I met my mother in a place I took to be England. I asked her how she had travelled from India to England, but she replied that she had come not from India but from Switzerland. In the second dream I dreamed that I saw my mother talking to a group of people. I approached her and spoke to her in Tibetan, but she did not seem to understand what I was saying. While she was alive my mother spoke only Tibetan, but in this dream she spoke English fluently. I asked her why she had forgotten Tibetan, but she did not reply. Later in the same dream I dreamed of a western couple who are helping with the development of Dharma Centres in Britain.

Both dreams seemed to give clues as to where my mother had been reborn. Two days after the second dream, the husband of the couple of whom I had dreamed visited me and told me that his wife was pregnant. I immediately remembered my dream and thought that her baby might be my mother's reincarnation. The fact that in the dream my mother had forgotten Tibetan and spoke only English suggested that she would be reborn in an English-speaking country, and the presence of this couple in the dream might have been an indication that they were her parents. I then performed a traditional divination together with ritual prayers, called a *mo* in Tibetan, and this indicated that their child was my mother's reincarnation. I was very happy but did not say anything to anyone.

On the night that the wife was taken to hospital to give birth I dreamed about my mother again and again. The next morning I considered the matter carefully and reached a decision. If her baby had been born that night then definitely it was my mother's reincarnation, but if it had not I would need to make further examinations. Having made this decision, I telephoned the husband who gave me the good news that his wife had given birth to a baby girl the previous night. I was delighted and performed a puja, or offering ceremony, as a thanksgiving to my Dharmapala.

A few days later, the father telephoned and told me that if he recited the mantra of Buddha Chenrezig, OM MANI PÄME HUM, when the baby cried she would immediately stop crying and appear to be listening to the mantra. He asked me why this was and I replied that it was because of her tendencies from her previous life. I knew that my mother had recited this mantra with strong faith throughout her life.

The child was named Amaravajra. Later, when Kuten Lama, my mother's brother, visited England and saw Amaravajra for the first time he was astonished by how affectionate she was towards him. He said that it was as if she recognised him. I also had the same experience. Although I am able to visit Amaravajra only very occasionally, she is always extremely happy to see me.

When Amaravajra started to talk, one day she pointed to a dog and said 'kyi, kyi'. After this she used to say 'kyi' many times whenever she saw a dog. Her father asked me if 'kyi' meant anything, and I told him that in the dialect of western Tibet, which is where my mother lived, 'kyi' means 'dog'. This was not the only Tibetan word the little girl uttered spontaneously.

I later heard through my sister's husband that after my mother's death a Tibetan astrologer had predicted that my mother would be born as a female in a country with a language other than Tibetan. This story is from my own personal experience, but if we investigate we can find many other true stories about how people have been able to recognize the reincarnations of their Teachers, parents, friends, and others. If we contemplate such stories and reflect on the nature of the mind and the experience of dreams we will definitely become convinced of the existence of past and future lives.

What is Karma?

To understand the laws that govern rebirth from one life to another we need to understand karma. 'Karma' is a Sanskrit term meaning 'action'. All intentional bodily, verbal, and mental actions are karma. Sometimes when Buddhists experience suffering or misfortune they say 'This is my karma', and accept it patiently. Strictly speaking, however, the suffering we experience is not actual karma but the effect of karma we have accumulated either in previous lives or earlier in this life.

All bodily and verbal actions depend upon mental actions because they are all preceded by a mental intention to act. Without an intention to act we would not do anything. A mental intention that is a determination to perform an action is a mental action or mental karma. Thus, bodily karma is bodily activity initiated by a mental action, and verbal karma is verbal activity initiated by a mental action. From this we can see that mental karma is more important than either bodily karma or verbal karma.

Whether an action is good, bad, or neutral depends principally upon the intention that motivates it. Good actions come from good intentions, bad actions from bad intentions, and neutral actions from neutral intentions. Good, or virtuous, actions are the main cause of rebirth in the higher realms, and of future happiness, whereas bad, or non-virtuous, actions are the main cause of rebirth in the lower realms, and of future suffering. This dependent relationship between actions and effects, virtuous

23

actions causing happiness and non-virtuous actions causing suffering, is taught by the Buddhas based on their perfect knowledge. We must believe in it because conviction in the laws of karma is the root of future happiness.

Every action we perform leaves an imprint on our very subtle mind, and each imprint eventually gives rise to its own effect. Our mind is like a field, and performing actions is like sowing seeds in that field. Virtuous actions sow seeds of future happiness and non-virtuous actions sow seeds of future suffering. These seeds remain dormant in our mind until the conditions for them to ripen occur, and then they produce their effect. In some cases this can happen many lifetimes after the original action was performed.

The seeds that ripen when we die are very important because they determine what kind of rebirth we will take in the next life. Which particular seed ripens at death depends upon the state of mind in which we die. If we die with a peaceful mind this will stimulate a virtuous seed and we will experience a fortunate rebirth, but if we die with an unpeaceful mind, such as in a state of anger, this will stimulate a non-virtuous seed and we will experience an unfortunate rebirth. This is similar to the way in which nightmares are triggered off by our being in an agitated state of mind just before falling asleep.

There are six realms in which it is possible to take rebirth: three lower realms and three higher realms. The three lower realms are the animal realm, the realm of the hungry ghosts, and the hell realm, and the three upper realms are the human realm, the demi-god realm, and the god realm. These are described in more detail in *A Meditation Handbook*.

Virtuous actions, or good karma, are the main cause not only of rebirth in the higher realms of humans and gods, but also of happiness and good fortune in general.

Thus if things go well for us in this life – if we have good health, comfortable living conditions, and good relationships with others, or if we meet with success in our activities – this is our previous good karma ripening. Similarly, success in our spiritual practice and all our spiritual attainments are the result of virtuous karma. Conversely, all the suffering we experience in this life, such as sickness, poverty, conflict, accidents, and harm from humans and non-humans, is the result of our own past negative karma. If our dearest wishes remain unfulfilled while the things we dislike appear with ease, or if we fail to find good friends, or, having found them, we are soon separated from them, these too are due to the ripening of our past negative karma. Even minor annoyances such as interferences in our daily routine, or the discontent that underlies so much of our life, are the result of the non-virtuous karma accumulated in previous lives.

From this we can see that if we want protection from suffering and from the danger of lower rebirth we must try not to commit any more negative karma; and we must also try to purify the negative karma that we have already committed. There are ten principal non-virtuous actions that we should avoid: three actions of the body, four of speech, and three of the mind. The three non-virtuous bodily actions are killing, stealing, and sexual misconduct; the four non-virtuous verbal actions are lying, divisive speech, hurtful speech, and idle chatter; and the three non-virtuous mental actions are covetousness, malice, and holding wrong views. These are explained fully in *Joyful Path of Good Fortune*.

The best way to avoid committing negative actions is to practise consideration for others. Since everyone, even animals and insects, wants to be happy and does not want to experience suffering, we should try never to harm any living being. If we kill even a tiny insect this is a non-virtuous action because it causes great suffering to the insect. We may enjoy fishing, but if we consider this action from the point of view of the fish we will realize how harmful it is. We need to develop compassion for humans and animals alike, without discrimination; and we should take the utmost care not to cause suffering to any living being.

All non-virtuous actions have three kinds of effect: the ripened effect, the effect similar to the cause, and the environmental effect. The ripened effect of a negative action is rebirth in one of the three lower realms. The most severe negative actions ripen as rebirth in the hell realm, less severe negative actions as rebirth in the hungry ghost realm, and the least severe negative actions as rebirth in the animal realm.

There are two kinds of effect that are similar to the cause: tendencies similar to the cause and experiences similar to the cause. These two effects are further repercussions of a non-virtuous action that are experienced after the ripened effect has finished and we have taken another rebirth in any of the six realms.

A tendency similar to the cause is a strong compulsion to repeat similar non-virtuous actions. This effect makes it very difficult for us to avoid committing further negative actions, and thereby creating the cause to take even more lower rebirths in the future. The tendency similar to the action of killing is to have a tendency to kill. For example, when some people see a spider in their room they automatically respond by crushing it, and there are some children who cannot resist tormenting or torturing animals. These are tendencies that resemble destructive actions committed in the past. Similarly, the tendency resembling the action of sexual misconduct is to feel strongly attracted to other people's partners.

The effects that are experiences similar to the ten non-virtuous actions are as follows. The experience similar to killing is that our life is short and full of sickness and disease. By killing we cut short the life of someone else and so we ourself experience a short life and ill health. If we are experiencing such things in this life we can know for certain that they are the results of our own previous negative actions. The experience similar to stealing is that we lack wealth and possessions, and when we do manage to gather some they are stolen from us or people borrow them and fail to return them. The experience similar to sexual misconduct is that we are quickly separated from our friends and family, our partners abandon us for someone else, the people who work for us soon resign, and we experience loneliness. We can see that some people who are old and ugly have many friends and devoted partners, while others who are young and beautiful cannot find a loyal partner or lasting friendships.

The experience similar to lying is that no one trusts what we say and people do not listen to our advice; the experience similar to divisive speech is that we find it hard to develop harmonious relationships with others; and the experience similar to hurtful speech is that others say unpleasant things to us and speak badly about us. Whenever someone hurts us by speaking offensively or sarcastically we can recognize this as the result of our own previous harsh words. The experience similar to idle chatter is that people do not take seriously what we say. They regard us as foolish and do not pay attention to our comments and opinions.

The experience similar to covetousness is that our desires are not fulfilled and we fail to obtain what we want; the experience similar to malice is that we are constantly prone to fear and we panic in dangerous situations; and the experience similar to holding wrong views is that we have great confusion and find it difficult to develop wisdom. Moreover, when we hear or read Dharma we are full of doubt. If we now find it hard to remove misconceptions and attain spiritual realizations this is the result of our clinging to wrong views in the past.

The third effect of a negative action is the environmental effect. Generally, this means that when we take another human rebirth, for example, our environment and the things that surround us are hostile, dangerous, or uncomfortable. The environmental effect of killing is that the place in which we live is poor and it is hard to find food and other necessities; the environmental effect of stealing is that the place in which we live is barren, and plants and crops will not flourish there; and the environmental effect of sexual misconduct is that the place in which we live is unclean and breeds disease.

The environmental effect of lying is that we live in a place where people cheat and deceive us, and where there is no one we can trust; and the environmental effect of divisive speech is that the place in which we live is rugged and mountainous, and there is little transport so people have to carry heavy loads. Since divisive speech makes smooth and harmonious relationships between people difficult and painful, we have to inhabit a hard and inhospitable environment where communications are difficult to establish. The environmental effect of hurtful speech is that we have to live in a place where there is dense undergrowth, or plants that sting and tear our flesh, causing us discomfort whenever we move about; and the environmental effect of idle chatter is that we live in a place where fruit and crops do not grow properly, or at the right time, and so they are wasted.

The environmental effect of covetousness is that we have to live in a place where material resources are easily destroyed or lost, or where our bodily strength and beauty quickly degenerate; the environmental effect of malice is that we are reborn in a place that is ravaged by war and disease, or where there is continuous conflict; and the environmental effect of holding wrong views is that we are reborn in a place that lacks water and resources are quickly exhausted. It is a place whe nothing precious exists – no works of art, no valuable treasures, no scriptures, no Spiritual Guides.

In the Buddhist scriptures it is said that if someone knows these effects and yet continues to commit non-virtuous actions, he or she is like someone with perfect eyesight who walks straight off the edge of a cliff! However, it is not enough merely to avoid committing such actions in the future – we also have to purify the negative karma we have accumulated in the past. If we do not purify past negative karma we will have to experience all these effects in the future, but if we practise purification we can prevent our negative karma from ripening at all. Out of his great compassion, Buddha taught many methods for purifying negative karma. Within these, one of the most powerful is the practice associated with the *Mahayana Sutra of the Three Superior Heaps*. This Sutra can be found in Appendix II of this book, and a detailed explanation of the practice can be found in the book *The Bodhisattva Vow*.

Buddha Jewel Moonlight

Buddha Meaningful to Behold   *Buddha Jewel Moon*

This Precious Human Life

As we have seen, it is possible to take rebirth in any one of the six realms, depending upon what kind of karma ripens when we die. This time we have taken rebirth as a human being, and so we now have the opportunity to enjoy all the advantages of a human life. If we contemplate these advantages we will realize that this life is very precious because it presents us with a unique opportunity for spiritual development. Compared to an animal life, for example, a human life generally affords many advantages such as good food, shelter, and freedom from predators; but the greatest advantage of being human is the special opportunity we have to develop our mind and thereby to free ourself and others from suffering.

A human life has almost limitless potential, but we will be able to realize this potential only if we first learn to appreciate it. Therefore we need to reflect again and again on the special opportunity we now have. If we develop a deep appreciation for the preciousness of this life we will definitely make a determination to use it wisely. Then we will feel as if our life has become truly meaningful.

Within our mind there are eighty-four thousand different delusions, all of which produce mental pain or inner disease. This inner disease has no beginning and, until we abandon our deluded states of mind, it will have no end. If we do not overcome our attachment, for example, it will remain in our mind like an insatiable thirst, constantly giving rise to feelings of dissatisfaction and frustration. Similarly, all the other delusions such as anger, jealousy, and selfishness will continue to cause us mental pain whenever they arise within our mind.

Even though we have been suffering from these inner diseases since time without beginning, we now have an opportunity to eradicate them completely. Buddha gave eighty-four thousand different instructions to cure these inner diseases and, unlike other living beings, humans have the opportunity to receive these instructions and put them into practice. Thus, by relying upon Buddha's teachings we can use our human life gradually to reduce and eventually to eradicate altogether our delusions, and all the pain and suffering to which they give rise.

Generally, there are three ways in which we can use our precious human life to realize its potential. We can use it to ensure that in future lives we will be born as a human with all the conditions necessary for a happy and meaningful life; we can use it to attain complete liberation from suffering; or we can use it to attain full enlightenment, or Buddhahood, for the sake of all living beings.

With a human mind, we can understand the existence of past and future lives. This understanding leads us to think beyond the preoccupations of this short life and to consider our welfare in future lives. We are led to the conclusion that if we want a good rebirth in the future we must create the causes for it now, in this life.

How can we do this? We can create the cause for a human rebirth in our next life by practising moral discipline in this life; we can create the cause to have an attractive body in that life by practising patience; and we can create the cause to enjoy abundant wealth and resources by practising giving. We can create the cause for our wishes to be fulfilled by engaging in virtuous actions with a joyful mind; we can create the cause to have a calm and peaceful mind by practising meditation;

and we can destroy our ignorance and solve all our inner problems by improving our wisdom. We can create the cause to enjoy good health and a long life by protecting life and helping the sick, and we can protect ourself from lower rebirth and ensure that we are reborn as a human or a god by making offerings, prostrations, and prayers to the Buddhas, Bodhisattvas, and other holy beings. In short, we can use this human life to create the cause for any good conditions we wish to experience in the future.

Non-humans such as animals do not have this opportunity, no matter how skilled they may be at other things. For example, some animals are very clever at hunting and finding food, and birds are very skilled at flying, but animals cannot practise moral discipline, or even develop the wish to practise it. All living beings, even worms and insects, can commit negative actions, but only humans have the opportunity to purify them. If we recite with faith the names of the Thirty-five Confession Buddhas in the *Mahayana Sutra of the Three Superior Heaps* we can swiftly purify even the heaviest negative karma.

However, even if we are reborn as a human in the next life, we will still not be free from suffering. All living beings within the six realms experience one problem after another. They have to endure the sufferings of birth, sickness, ageing, death, disappointment, frustration, and so forth again and again, in life after life. This cycle of uncontrolled death and rebirth pervaded by suffering is called 'samsara'. As humans, we can understand how we are trapped in samsara, what causes us to take rebirth in samsara, and how we can escape from it. With this understanding we will naturally develop a wish to escape from samsara and attain permanent freedom from suffering. This wish is called 'renunciation'. If, with this motivation, we engage in the spiritual practices of moral discipline, concentration, and wisdom that are explained in Part Two of this book, we will eventually eradicate all our delusions and attain complete liberation from samsara and all its problems.

Complete liberation from the delusions and suffering, however, is not the greatest goal we can accomplish with this human life. If we consider the plight of others we will see that all living beings are trapped in samsara, experiencing terrible suffering in life after life, and if we then rely upon Buddha's Mahayana teachings we will be able to develop great compassion for all these suffering beings. Seeing that the only way we can protect them from suffering is to develop all the skills and qualities of a Buddha, we will make a strong determination to become a Buddha for the sake of all living beings. This special mind is called 'bodhichitta', or the 'mind of enlightenment'. Once we develop bodhichitta we become a Bodhisattva and enter into the Bodhisattva's way of life. The essence of the Bodhisattva's way of life is the practice of the six perfections – the perfections of giving, moral discipline, patience, effort, mental stabilization, and wisdom. These are explained in Part Three of this book. If we practise the six perfections sincerely, eventually we will attain full enlightenment and become a Conqueror Buddha.

Just as Prince Siddhartha used his human life to practise Dharma and attain full enlightenment, so can we use our precious human life to do the same. If we realize that this precious human life has such great potential we will feel extremely fortunate, and we will decide not to waste it on meaningless activities but to extract its essence by practising pure Dharma.

What is Meditation?

The heart of Dharma practice is meditation. The purpose of meditation is to make our mind calm and peaceful. If our mind is peaceful we will be free from worries and mental discomfort, and so we will experience true happiness; but if our mind is not peaceful we will find it very difficult to be happy, even if we are living in the very best conditions. If we train in meditation our mind will gradually become more and more peaceful, and we will experience a purer and purer form of happiness. Eventually we will be able to stay happy all the time, even in the most difficult circumstances.

Usually we find it difficult to control our mind. It seems as if our mind is like a balloon in the wind – blown here and there by external circumstances. If things go well our mind is happy, but if they go badly it immediately becomes unhappy. For example, if we get what we want, such as a new possession or a new partner, we become excited and cling to them tightly; but since we cannot have everything we want, and since we will inevitably be separated from the friends and possessions we currently enjoy, this mental stickiness, or attachment, serves only to cause us pain. On the other hand, if we do not get what we want, or if we lose something that we like, we become despondent or irritated. For example, if we are forced to work with a colleague whom we dislike we will probably become irritated and feel aggrieved, with the result that we will be unable to work with them efficiently and our time at work will become stressful and unrewarding.

Such fluctuations of mood arise because we are too closely involved in the external situation. We are like a child making a sand castle who is excited when it is first made, but who becomes upset when it is destroyed by the incoming tide. By training in meditation we create an inner space and clarity that enables us to control our mind regardless of the external circumstances. Gradually we develop mental equilibrium, a balanced mind that is happy all the time, rather than an unbalanced mind that oscillates between the extremes of excitement and despondency.

If we train in meditation systematically, eventually we will be able to eradicate from our mind the delusions that are the causes of all our problems and suffering. In this way we will come to experience a permanent inner peace, known as 'liberation' or 'nirvana'. Then, day and night in life after life we will experience only peace and happiness.

Meditation is a method for acquainting our mind with virtue. It is a mind that analyzes or concentrates on a virtuous object. A virtuous object is one that causes us to develop a peaceful mind when we analyze it or concentrate on it. If we contemplate an object and it causes us to develop an unpeaceful mind such as anger or attachment, this indicates that that object is non-virtuous. There are also many objects that are neither virtuous nor non-virtuous, but neutral.

There are two types of meditation: analytical meditation and placement meditation. Analytical meditation involves contemplating the meaning of a Dharma instruction that we have heard or read. By contemplating such instructions deeply, eventually we reach a definite conclusion, or cause a specific virtuous state of mind to arise. This is the object of placement meditation. We then concentrate single-pointedly on this conclusion or virtuous state of mind for as long as possible so as to become deeply acquainted with it. This single-pointed concentration is placement meditation. Generally, the term 'meditation' is used to refer to placement meditation, while analytical meditation is often referred to simply as 'contemplation'. Placement meditation depends upon analytical meditation, and analytical meditation depends upon listening to or reading Dharma instructions.

The first stage of meditation is to stop distractions and make our mind clearer and more lucid. This can be accomplished by practising a simple breathing meditation. We choose a quiet place to meditate and sit in a comfortable position. We can sit in the traditional cross-legged posture or in any other position that is comfortable. If we wish, we can sit in a chair. The most important thing is to keep our back straight to prevent our mind from becoming sluggish or sleepy.

We sit with our eyes partially closed and turn our attention to our breathing. We breathe naturally, preferably through the nostrils, without attempting to control our breath, and we try to become aware of the sensation of the breath as it enters and leaves the nostrils. This sensation is our object of meditation. We should try to concentrate on it to the exclusion of everything else.

At first our mind will be very busy, and we might even feel that the meditation is making our mind busier; but in reality we are just becoming more aware of how busy our mind actually is. There will be a great temptation to follow the different thoughts as they arise, but we should resist this and remain focused single-pointedly on the sensation of the breath. If we discover that our mind has wandered and is following our thoughts we should immediately return it to the breath. We should repeat this as many times as necessary until the mind settles on the breath.

If we practise patiently in this way, gradually our distracting thoughts will subside and we will experience a sense of inner peace and relaxation. Our mind will feel lucid and spacious and we will feel refreshed. When the sea is rough, sediment is churned up and the water becomes murky, but when the wind dies down the mud gradually settles and the water becomes clear. In a similar way, when the otherwise incessant flow of our distracting thoughts is calmed through concentrating on the breath, our mind becomes unusually lucid and clear. We should stay with this state of mental calm for a while.

Even though breathing meditation is only a preliminary stage of meditation, it can be quite powerful. We can see from this practice that it is possible to experience inner peace and contentment just by controlling the mind, without having to depend at all upon external conditions. When the turbulence of distracting thoughts subsides and our mind becomes still, a deep happiness and contentment arises naturally from within. This feeling of contentment and well-being helps us to cope with the busyness and difficulties of daily life. So much of the stress and tension we normally experience comes from our mind, and many of the problems we experience, including ill health, are caused or aggravated by this stress. Just by doing breathing meditation for ten or fifteen minutes each day, we will be able to reduce this stress. We will experience a calm, spacious feeling in the mind, and many of our usual problems will fall away. Difficult situations will become easier to deal with, we will naturally feel warm and well-disposed towards other people, and our relationships with others will gradually improve.

We should train in this preliminary meditation until we gain some experience of it; but if we want to attain permanent, unchanging inner peace, and if we want to become completely free from problems and suffering, we will need to advance beyond simple breathing meditation to more practical forms of meditation, such as the cycle of twenty-one meditations explained in *A Meditation*

Handbook. When we do these meditations we begin by calming the mind with breathing meditation as just explained, and then we proceed to the stages of analytical and placement meditation according to the specific instructions for each meditation. Some of these meditations will now be introduced in this book.

Buddha Stainless One

Buddha Bestower of Glory *Buddha Pure One*

Death

Everyone is aware of the fact that sooner or later they will die, but for most of us this is just a superficial awareness. Deep down we habitually assume that our death will not occur until some time in the distant future. All the time in the back of our mind there is the tacit assumption that we will not die today. Even on the day on which we actually die we will probably be assuming that we will not die and be making plans for the next day! We live our life as if we were going to remain in this world forever, and consequently we devote almost all of our time to the affairs of this life and think little about what will happen after we die.

Our preoccupation with trivial, mundane activities causes us to waste our precious human life. Instead of using it to accomplish one of the three great goals mentioned earlier, we use it only to obtain food, clothing, and shelter, to acquire material possessions, to indulge in sex and other superficial pleasures, and to seek promotion and high social status. In this respect we are no different from animals who scavenge for food, make shelters, produce young, protect their territory, and vie for supremacy within the herd or flock.

A human life such as ours is extremely rare and difficult to obtain, so what a great tragedy it would be if instead of using it to advance spiritually we were to waste it by living like an animal. The best way to avoid wasting this precious life is to become acutely aware of our impermanence by meditating on death.

We meditate on death to acquaint our mind with three thoughts:

1 I will definitely die.
2 The time of my death is utterly uncertain.
3 At the time of my death and after my death only the practice of Dharma will help me.

We need to meditate on these thoughts again and again in analytical meditation until we develop a deep experience of them and they come to affect the way we live our life. To acquaint ourself with the first thought, we can contemplate three lines of reasoning:

1 I will definitely die because there is no way to prevent my body from finally decaying.
2 Day by day, moment by moment, my life is slipping away.
3 My death will come regardless of whether or not I have made the time to practise Dharma.

By contemplating these points we come to a clear conclusion: 'I will definitely die', and we meditate on this conclusion in placement meditation. We then contemplate the following three points:

1 I have no idea when I will die. I may be young and healthy, but this does not mean that I will not die soon. Many young people die before their parents. There is no certainty in this world.
2 There are so many causes of untimely death. For example, many strong and healthy people die as a result of unforeseen accidents.
3 This human body is extremely fragile and can easily be destroyed, even by the smallest of objects.

Through contemplating these points we will realize that the time of our death is completely uncertain and that we have absolutely no guarantee that we will not die today. When we are convinced of this we should mentally repeat over and over again 'I may die today, I may die today', and concentrate on the feeling it evokes.

Then we contemplate the following three points:

1 At the time of my death my wealth and possessions will be of no benefit to me.
2 At the time of my death my family and friends will not be able to help me.
3 At the time of my death even my body will be of no use to me.

By contemplating these points we realize that at the time of our death and after our death only Dharma practice will help us, and we meditate on this conclusion.

Finally, we conclude our contemplations by making three resolutions:

I will practise Dharma
I will practise Dharma right now
I will practise Dharma purely

and we meditate on these determinations without distraction for as long as we can. We should put these resolutions into practice and integrate them into our daily life. By doing this, we can protect ourself from the dangers of lower rebirth, attain a permanent cessation of all suffering, and even accomplish full enlightenment.

The Buddhist Way of Life

Although we have taken a human rebirth in this life, this does not mean that we will always be a human. Until we have thoroughly purified our mind, it is quite possible that after we die we will be reborn as an animal, as a hungry ghost, or as a hell being. However, if we rely sincerely upon Buddha, Dharma, and Sangha we will protect ourself from the danger of lower rebirth, and from all other dangers.

Buddha, Dharma, and Sangha are called the 'Three Jewels' because they are very precious. If we realize the danger we are in, develop complete confidence in the power of the Three Jewels to protect us, and then make a heartfelt determination to rely upon the Three Jewels for the rest of our life, at that moment we enter the Buddhist path and become a Buddhist. Once we become a Buddhist we have the opportunity to accomplish all the spiritual realizations of the Buddhist path, from the realization of relying upon a Spiritual Guide through to the path of No More Learning, or Buddhahood.

From this we can see that there are two main causes of going for refuge to the Three Jewels: realizing the danger we are in and developing conviction in the power of the Three Jewels to protect us from this danger. To generate the first cause in our mind we need to become convinced of the possibility of our being reborn as an animal, a hungry ghost, or a hell being. We can do this by considering the following reasoning. When we die our mind has to leave this present body, which is just a temporary abode, and find another body, rather like a bird leaving one nest to fly to another. Our mind has no freedom to remain and no choice about where to go. We are blown to the place of our next rebirth by the winds of our karma. If the karma that ripens at our deathtime is negative, we will definitely take a lower rebirth. Heavy negative karma causes rebirth in hell, less negative karma causes rebirth as a hungry ghost, and the least negative karma causes rebirth as an animal.

It is very easy to commit heavy negative karma. For example, simply by swatting a mosquito out of anger we create the cause to be reborn in hell. Throughout this and all our countless previous lives we have committed many heavy negative actions. Unless we have already purified these actions by practising sincere confession, their potentialities will remain on our mental continuum, and any one of these negative potentialities could ripen when we die. Bearing this in mind, we should think:

> *If I die today where will I be tomorrow? It is quite possible that I will find myself in the animal realm, among the hungry ghosts, or in hell. If someone were to call me a stupid cow today I would find it difficult to bear, but what will I do if I actually become a cow, a pig, or a fish?*

We should contemplate this until we generate a strong fear of taking rebirth in the lower realms. This fear is the first main cause of going for refuge to the Three Jewels. More reasons establishing the possibility of rebirth in the lower realms can be found in *Joyful Path of Good Fortune*.

To develop the other main cause of going for refuge – a conviction that Buddha, Dharma, and Sangha have complete power to protect living beings from lower rebirth – we should contemplate as follows. The actual refuge is Dharma. As mentioned earlier, Dharma is Buddha's teachings and our own inner experience of these teachings. It is our Dharma, our own spiritual realizations, that directly protects us from taking rebirth in the lower realms. How is this? The cause of lower rebirth is negative actions, which we commit because our mind is under the influence of delusions. By practising Buddha's teachings we become familiar with special, virtuous states of mind that are the direct opposite of these delusions. As our virtuous minds become more powerful, our delusions naturally become weaker. For example, as our experience of love increases, our hatred decreases, and as our ability to rejoice in others' good fortune improves, our jealousy diminishes. As our negative minds become weaker, we stop committing the negative karma that causes us to take rebirth in the lower realms. This is how our inner experience of Dharma protects us from the danger of lower rebirth.

If we train in the more advanced Buddhist practices described later in this book, particularly in wisdom realizing emptiness, eventually we will gain a direct experience of ultimate truth, emptiness, and thereby permanently eradicate all our delusions. Once our mind is completely free from delusions we will be liberated from all suffering forever.

Whereas Dharma is the actual refuge, Buddha is the source of all refuge. He is the supreme Spiritual Guide who shows us the way to attain Dharma realizations and who sustains our Dharma practice by bestowing his blessings. The Sangha are the supreme spiritual friends who support our Dharma practice. They provide conducive conditions, encourage us in our practice, and set a good example for us to follow. Only the Three Jewels have the ability to protect living beings from all suffering.

If we contemplate these points carefully we will generate a strong conviction that Buddha, Dharma, and Sangha have complete power to protect living beings from lower rebirth and from all fear and suffering. This conviction is the second main cause of going for refuge. With these two main causes firmly established in our mind, we should pray every day to the Three Jewels by reciting the following refuge prayer:

All Buddhas, Bodhisattvas, and holy beings,
Please protect me and all living beings
From the various sufferings, fears, and dangers of
    samsara.
Please bestow your blessings upon our body and
    mind.

In this prayer, 'Buddhas' refers to the Buddha Jewel, and 'Bodhisattvas and holy beings' to the Sangha Jewel, the assembly of Superior beings who have realized ultimate truth directly. When we recite this verse, we imagine that in front of us is the living Buddha Shakyamuni, surrounded by all the Buddhas and Bodhisattvas, like the full moon surrounded by stars. We generate a strong conviction that all these holy beings are actually present before us and develop strong faith in them.

When we recite the words 'Please protect me' while concentrating on their meaning, we are familiarizing our mind with renunciation, the wish to release ourself from the various sufferings, fears, and dangers of samsara; and when we recite 'and all living beings' we are familiarizing our mind with great compassion, the wish to release all other living beings from these sufferings, fears, and dangers. When we recite the last line, we are requesting the Buddhas, Bodhisattvas, and other holy beings to bless us so that the realizations of renunciation and great compassion will grow within our mind. These realizations are Dharma Jewels.

In summary, by reciting this verse while contemplating its meaning we are establishing within our mind the special Dharma Jewels of the realizations of renunciation and great compassion by receiving the blessings of the Buddha Jewel and the Sangha Jewel. This is the real meaning of going for refuge to the Three Jewels. If we are able to remember this practice when we die we will definitely be protected from rebirth in the lower realms.

The foundation of the Buddhist way of life is to go for refuge to the Three Jewels from the depths of our heart every day, and to keep purely the twelve commitments of going for refuge. These are explained in Appendix I. The essential meaning of these commitments is that we should have complete faith and confidence in the Three Jewels and live in accordance with the laws of karma – abandoning non-virtuous actions such as killing and stealing, and practising virtuous actions such as maintaining a compassionate mind towards humans and animals alike. Anyone who wishes to follow the Buddhist path should become thoroughly familiar with these twelve commitments.

PART TWO

The Path to Liberation

Buddha Transforming with Purity

Buddha Water Deity   *Buddha God of Water Deities*

What is Liberation?

Liberation is a permanent inner peace attained through the complete abandonment of delusions. When through training in the paths to liberation our mind is completely released from delusions, the ultimate nature of our mind becomes a liberation, or a nirvana. From that moment on we are free from samsara and all its sufferings, and we have become a Foe Destroyer, a person who has destroyed the inner enemies of attachment, hatred, and self-grasping ignorance.

As mentioned earlier, forty-nine days after Buddha had attained enlightenment he was requested by Brahma and Indra to turn the Wheel of Dharma. The first teaching Buddha gave was the *Sutra of the Four Noble Truths* in which he explained about true sufferings, true origins, true cessations, and true paths. Samsaric rebirth, such as our present rebirth, is called 'true suffering' because it is the basis of all other suffering and delusions; and delusions and actions motivated by delusions are called 'true origins' because they are the origin, or source, of all sufferings. Liberation is called a 'true cessation' because it is a permanent cessation of delusions and sufferings, and the paths that lead to liberation are called 'true paths' because by following these paths we attain true cessations. Buddha said:

You should know sufferings.
You should abandon origins.
You should attain cessations.
You should meditate on paths.

51

The meaning of this is that we should first understand that samsaric rebirth is the nature of suffering and develop renunciation for it. Then we should abandon the delusions and negative actions that are the source, or origin, of samsaric rebirth and all its sufferings; and make our human life truly meaningful by attaining liberation. To attain this permanent cessation of suffering we should practise the paths to liberation.

The four noble truths can be understood and practised on many different levels. Directly or indirectly, all Dharma practices are included within the practice of the four noble truths. At a basic level we can begin the practice of the four noble truths by reflecting on the sufferings caused by anger. Anger destroys both peace of mind and peace in the world. The root cause of the two world wars and of all the wars being fought in various parts of the world today is anger. On a smaller scale, anger destroys our personal relationships, our reputation, and the harmony within families and communities. Most of the arguments and most of the day-to-day difficulties we experience with our family, friends, and colleagues are due to anger. The root of all our future happiness is our virtuous karmic potentialities, the positive energy produced by our past virtuous actions that we carry in our mental continuum. Anger destroys these potentialities and thereby robs us of the good effects of our virtuous actions. Moreover, through causing us to commit heavy negative actions, anger can even throw us into the fires of hell in future lives. Nothing harms us more than anger.

Recognizing the terrible and unnecessary sufferings that arise from anger, we should develop renunciation for them and then strive to abandon their cause, the mind of anger, by practising patience. In this way we can attain a cessation of anger. The sufferings caused by anger are true sufferings, anger itself is a true origin, the practice of patience is a practice of true paths, and the permanent cessation of anger is a true cessation. We can also apply the same principles to the sufferings caused by attachment and ignorance.

Buddha Glorious Excellence

Buddha Glorious Sandalwood   *Buddha Endless Splendour*

Developing Renunciation

Wherever we are born in samsara, even in the highest god realm, there is no freedom from suffering. Certainly the human realm is not free from suffering. We have only to look around us, read a newspaper, or watch television, to see that human beings experience terrible sufferings. Moreover, if we succeed in taking rebirth in the fortunate realms it is only like taking a short holiday. Afterwards we once again have to descend to the lower realms, where we experience extreme suffering for inconceivably long periods. We experience all these sufferings because we are in samsara. If we think deeply about this we will realize that if we want real freedom and real happiness we must escape from samsara.

To escape from samsara we must cut its root by eradicating self-grasping from our mental continuum. This depends upon training in higher wisdom, which depends upon training in higher concentration, which depends upon training in higher moral discipline. These three trainings are called 'higher trainings' because they are motivated by renunciation. Therefore, our first step in escaping from samsara is to develop renunciation.

We develop renunciation by contemplating the many faults of samsara such as those set out below. We may wonder why it is necessary to contemplate sufferings such as birth, ageing, sickness, and death, especially since we have already experienced the first and can do nothing to avoid the others. The reason is that by meditating on these sufferings we realize that the very nature of samsaric existence is suffering, and that until we escape from samsara we will have to experience the same pains in life after life. This induces a strong wish to escape from samsara by abandoning its cause, self-grasping. This wish is renunciation.

There now follow seven separate contemplations on the sufferings of samsara. It is not necessary to contemplate all these points every time we meditate. Rather we should contemplate mainly those points that have the greatest impact on our mind and that help us to develop renunciation. When a strong feeling of renunciation arises in our mind we should refrain from further analysis and focus our mind single-pointedly on this feeling for as long as possible.

In these contemplations we think about the various sufferings experienced in the human realm, but we should bear in mind that the sufferings of other realms are generally far worse.

BIRTH

We have to spend the first nine months of our life cramped inside our mother's womb. At the beginning the rapid growth of our limbs makes us feel as if we are being stretched out on a rack, and in the later months of pregnancy we feel as if we are squashed inside a small water tank full of filthy liquid. We are extremely sensitive to everything our mother does. For example, if she runs, our fragile body is severely jolted, and if she drinks anything hot it feels like boiling water scalding our skin. During all this time we are completely alone. Our mother does not know the suffering and fear that we experience and, even if she did, she would be powerless to help us.

When we finally emerge from the womb it is like being forced through a narrow crevice between two hard rocks into a harsh and alien world. We have forgotten all we knew in our previous life, and have no way of understanding what is now happening to us. It is as if we are blind, deaf, and dumb. Our skin is so tender that even the softest clothes feel abrasive. When we are hungry we cannot say 'I need food', and when we are in pain we cannot say 'This is hurting me'. The only signs we can make are hot tears and furious gestures. We are completely helpless and have to be taught everything – how to eat, how to sit, how to walk, how to talk.

AGEING

As we grow old, our youthful vitality diminishes. We become bent, ugly, and burdened with illness. Our eyesight grows weaker and our hearing fails. We cannot derive the same enjoyment from the things we used to enjoy, such as food, drink, and sex. We are too weak to play games, and we are often too exhausted even for entertainments. When we are young we can travel around the whole world, but when we are old we can hardly walk to our own front door. We become too weak to engage in many worldly activities and our spiritual activities are often curtailed. For example, we cannot make many prostrations or travel far to receive teachings. If we meditate it becomes harder for us to gain realizations because our memory and concentration are weak and we find it difficult to stay awake. Our intellect is less sharp than it was during our youth, and so when we try to study it takes much longer to understand things.

Unable to do the work we used to do, or to help others in the way we would like to, we begin to feel useless to society and start to lose our self-respect. We are often neglected by our own children, and we watch helplessly as one by one our friends and contemporaries grow sick and die. Inexorably our loneliness deepens. If we did not practise Dharma while we were younger and had the opportunity, we pass our few remaining years with a growing fear of death and a deepening sense of regret for a wasted life.

SICKNESS

Having been born human, it is almost impossible to escape having to experience sickness in this life. When we fall ill we are like a bird that has been soaring in the sky and is suddenly shot down. When a bird is shot, it falls straight to the ground like a lump of lead and all its glory and power are immediately destroyed. Even a mild illness can be completely incapacitating. We cannot enjoy the food we like or take part in the activities of our friends. We may be told that we must never again eat our favourite food, drink alcohol, or engage in strenuous exercise. If our disease is more serious we may have to undergo painful and possibly risky operations. Should these fail, we will be told that the doctors can do nothing to cure us and we have only a short time left to live. If we have not used our life to practise Dharma we will be overcome by fear and regret.

Young people in their prime may be struck down by an incurable degenerative illness and, though they remain alive for many years, they will have to watch themselves slowly deteriorate. Realizing that their most treasured hopes and dreams will never be fulfilled they may wish they could die sooner. When we hear or read about the horrible diseases experienced by others we must remember that the same could happen to us. While we remain in samsara we are never safe from the threat of sickness.

DEATH

If during our life we have worked hard to acquire possessions and have become very attached to them, we will experience great suffering when we are separated from them at the time of death. Even now we find it difficult to lend one of our most treasured possessions to someone else, let alone to give it away. No wonder we become so miserable when we realize that in the hands of death we must abandon everything.

When we die we have to part from even our closest friends. We have to leave our partner, even though we may have been together for many years and never spent a day apart. If we are very attached to our friends we will experience great misery at the time of death, but all we will be able to do is to hold their hands. We will not be able to halt the process of death, even if they plead with us not to die. Usually when we are very attached to someone we feel jealous if they leave us on our own and spend time with someone else, but when we die we will have to leave our friends with others forever. If we have children we will have to leave them when we die. We will have to leave our spiritual friends and all the people who have helped us in this life.

When we die, this body that we have cherished and cared for in so many ways will have to be left behind. It will become mindless like a stone and will be buried in the ground or cremated. If we have not practised Dharma and cultivated virtuous actions, at the time of death we will develop fear and distress, as well as bodily pain.

HAVING TO PART WITH WHAT WE LIKE

Before the final separation at the time of death, we often have to experience temporary separation from the people and things we like. We may have to leave our country where all our friends and relatives live, or we may have to leave the job we like. We may lose our reputation. Many times in this life we have to experience the misery of parting from the people we like, or forsaking and losing the things we find pleasant and attractive, but when we die we have to part forever from all the companions and enjoyments of this life.

HAVING TO ENCOUNTER WHAT WE DO NOT LIKE

We are often forced to live or work with people we find unpleasant, such as those who criticize us for no reason, or with those who continually interfere with our wishes. Sometimes we may find ourself in very dangerous situations such as in a fire or an earthquake, or attacked by a mugger or a rapist. If our country goes to war we may be called up to fight, or be imprisoned if we refuse. Our homes may be bombed and our relatives killed. Our lives are full of less extreme situations which we find annoying. On holiday it rains, but back in the office the heat is stifling. Our business fails, or we lose our job, or we use up all our savings. We argue with our partner, our children cause us many worries, and old friends suddenly turn against us. Whatever we do, something always seems to go wrong. Even in our Dharma practice we continually meet obstacles. When we sit down to meditate we are distracted by outside noise, the telephone rings, or someone comes to see us. Sometimes it seems that even though we have been practising for years our delusions are stronger than ever. Even though we try so hard to be considerate, sometimes our family or our friends become unhappy about our Dharma practice. It is as if we are living in a thorn bush – whenever we adjust ourself to make ourself more comfortable, the thorns only pierce us more deeply. In samsara, aggravation and frustration are the natural state of affairs.

FAILING TO SATISFY OUR DESIRES

We have countless desires. Many cannot be fulfilled at all and others, when fulfilled, do not bring us the satisfaction for which we hoped. Many people are unable to satisfy even modest desires for the basic necessities of life such as adequate food, clothing, shelter, companionship, tolerable work, or a degree of personal freedom. Unfortunately, even if these basic needs are met, our desires do not end there. Soon we need a car, a more luxurious home, a better-paid job. In the past a simple holiday at the seaside may have been sufficient, but our expectations continually increase and now we need expensive, foreign holidays.

Ambition and competitiveness are a common cause of dissatisfaction. The ambitious schoolchild cannot rest content until he or she comes top of the class, nor the businessman until he has made his fortune. Clearly not everyone can come top. For one person to win, others must lose. But even the winners are rarely satisfied for long; their ambition drives them on until they too are beaten, worn out, or dead.

Another reason why we fail to satisfy all our desires is that they are often contradictory. For example, we may want both worldly success and a simple life, or fame and privacy, or rich food and a slim figure, or excitement and security. We may demand our own way all the time and still expect to be popular, or we may wish for Dharma realizations yet still covet a good reputation and material wealth. Our desires often involve other people and this creates special complications. Many relationships break up because of unrealistic expectations and desires.

We seek perfection – the perfect society, the perfect home, the perfect partner – but perfection cannot be found in samsara. Samsara promises much but can never deliver real satisfaction. It is not possible for impure, transient objects to provide the lasting joy we seek. This can be attained only by thoroughly purifying our mind. Though ignorance is the fundamental cause, worldly desires are the fuel that perpetuates the fire of samsara;

therefore we need to reduce our worldly desires by recognizing their faults.

By contemplating these seven types of suffering we will come to the following conclusion:

I have experienced these sufferings over and over again in the past and, if I do not attain liberation, I shall have to experience them over and over again in the future. Therefore I must escape from samsara.

When this thought arises clearly and definitely in our mind we do placement meditation.

If we do this meditation again and again, eventually the wish to attain liberation from samsara will arise spontaneously day and night. At that time we will have attained the actual realization of renunciation and entered the actual path to liberation. Every action motivated by renunciation is a cause for attaining liberation.

If we have some experience of renunciation we can transform our everyday activities into the path to liberation by maintaining the intention to benefit others and mentally dedicating the virtue of our actions to our own and others' liberation from samsara. When we meet with difficult circumstances or see others experiencing difficulties, we should use this to remind ourself of the disadvantages of samsara. When things are going well we should not be deceived but recall that samsaric pleasures are short-lived and ensnare us if we become attached to them. In this way we can use all our experiences of daily life to strengthen our determination to leave samsara and attain liberation.

The Three Higher Trainings

As mentioned before, the actual paths to liberation from samsara are the three higher trainings: higher moral discipline, higher concentration, and higher wisdom. They are called 'higher' trainings because they are practised with the motivation of renunciation. To attain liberation we need to abandon self-grasping, the root of samsara, by attaining a special wisdom directly realizing emptiness, or selflessness. This attainment depends upon a special type of concentration known as 'tranquil abiding', which in turn depends upon pure moral discipline. Moral discipline helps to pacify our distractions, the main obstacle to attaining the concentration of tranquil abiding; tranquil abiding makes our mind stable, lucid, and powerful; and wisdom realizing emptiness directly opposes self-grasping ignorance. Therefore, if we practise moral discipline, concentration, and wisdom with the motivation of renunciation we will definitely be able to destroy our self-grasping and attain liberation from samsara.

TRAINING IN HIGHER MORAL DISCIPLINE

In general, moral discipline is a virtuous mental determination to abandon any fault, or a bodily or verbal action motivated by such a determination. We practise moral discipline whenever we put this determination into practice. If our practice of moral discipline is not motivated by renunciation it will cause us to attain higher rebirth

Buddha Glorious Light

Buddha Glorious One
without Sorrow

Buddha Son
without Craving

within samsara, such as rebirth as a human or a god; but if it is motivated by renunciation it will lead to the attainment of liberation from samsara. This is why moral discipline practised with the motivation of renunciation is called 'higher moral discipline'. Higher moral discipline is an actual path to liberation. The pure practices of the ordination vows, the Bodhisattva vows, and the Tantric vows are all included within training in higher moral discipline, and all are paths to liberation.

TRAINING IN HIGHER CONCENTRATION

Pure concentration is a mind whose nature is to be single-pointedly placed on a virtuous object and whose function is to prevent distraction. Concentration practised with the motivation of renunciation is higher concentration and is an actual path to liberation. Whenever we engage in meditation with the motivation of renunciation we are training in higher concentration.

There are many levels of concentration. To attain a direct realization of emptiness, the ultimate nature of reality, we need the concentration of tranquil abiding. Tranquil abiding is a concentration that possesses a special type of suppleness attained by progressing through nine levels of concentration called the 'nine mental abidings'. When we have attained tranquil abiding our mind is very stable, clear, and powerful, and so it is very easy for us to attain Dharma realizations. A detailed explanation of how to attain tranquil abiding can be found in *Joyful Path of Good Fortune*.

TRAINING IN HIGHER WISDOM

In general, wisdom is a virtuous mind that functions mainly to dispel doubt and confusion by understanding its object thoroughly. Among the many different types of wisdom, the wisdom that realizes emptiness, the ultimate nature of phenomena, is supreme. Whenever we meditate on emptiness with the motivation of renunciation we are training in higher wisdom. Through training in higher wisdom, eventually our mind will be released from all delusions, including self-grasping ignorance, and we will attain liberation from samsara.

Anyone who practises these three higher trainings is said to be 'maintaining Buddhadharma by means of realization'. There are two ways to maintain Buddhadharma: by means of scripture and by means of realization. We maintain Buddhadharma by means of scripture when we listen to, read, or study Dharma, and we maintain Buddhadharma by means of realization when we actually put these instructions into practice and gain realizations.

PART THREE

The Path to Enlightenment

Buddha Glorious Flower

*Buddha Clearly Knowing
through Enjoying
Pure Radiance*

*Buddha Clearly Knowing
through Enjoying
Lotus Radiance*

Becoming a Bodhisattva

As already explained, the most meaningful use to which we can put our precious human life is not to attain liberation from suffering for ourself, but to attain great enlightenment, or Buddhahood, for the sake of all living beings. To do this we must rely upon Buddha's Mahayana teachings. First we generate the special motivation of bodhichitta and then we enter into the Bodhisattva's way of life and engage in the practice of the six perfections, until eventually, by completing this training, we become an enlightened being, a Buddha.

Bodhichitta is a primary mind motivated by great compassion that wishes to attain full enlightenment for the benefit of all living beings. This special mind does not arise naturally but has to be cultivated in meditation for a long time. Eventually, through the force of familiarity, it becomes spontaneous, arising naturally day and night without effort. When this happens we become a Bodhisattva, a being bound for enlightenment.

If we train in bodhichitta and follow the Bodhisattva's way of life, eventually our mind will be released from both the delusions and the imprints of the delusions. Delusions are called 'obstructions to liberation' because they keep us in samsara, and the imprints of the delusions are called 'obstructions to omniscience' because they prevent us from attaining a simultaneous and direct cognition of all phenomena. When our mind is completely free from both obstructions, the ultimate nature of our mind becomes a full enlightenment, a great liberation, or a great nirvana, and we ourself become a Conqueror Buddha.

The root of bodhichitta is great compassion, an unbiased compassion that wishes to protect all living beings without exception from suffering. We can develop great compassion only if we first develop affectionate love for all living beings. Affectionate love is a mind that feels close to others and holds them dear. If we love others we naturally feel compassion for them when we become aware of their suffering. Therefore, to become a Bodhisattva we must first develop affectionate love for all living beings, and then generate great compassion and bodhichitta.

AFFECTIONATE LOVE

Buddha taught that to develop affectionate love for all living beings we should learn to recognize them as our mothers and contemplate their kindness. To do this we should contemplate as follows. Since it is impossible to find a beginning to our mental continuum, it follows that we have taken countless rebirths in the past, and if we have had countless rebirths we must have had countless mothers. Where are all these mothers now? They are all the living beings alive today.

It is incorrect to reason that our mothers of former lives are no longer our mothers just because a long time has passed since they actually cared for us. If our present mother were to die today, would she cease to be our mother? No, we would still regard her as our mother and pray for her happiness. The same is true of all our previous mothers – they died, yet they remain our mothers. It is only because of the changes in our external appearance that we do not recognize each other.

In our daily life, we see many different living beings, both human and non-human. We regard some as friends, some as enemies, and most as strangers. These distinctions are made by our mistaken minds; they are not verified by valid minds. As a result of the different karmic relationships we have had in the past, some living beings now appear to us to be attractive, some unattractive, and others neither particularly attractive nor unattractive. We tend to assent to these appearances unquestioningly, as if they were really true. We believe that those who now appear pleasant are intrinsically pleasant people, while those whom we find unattractive are actually unpleasant. This way of thinking is clearly incorrect. If the people whom we find attractive were intrinsically pleasant, everyone who met them would find them pleasant; and if the people whom we find unattractive were intrinsically unpleasant, everyone who met them would find them unpleasant; but this is not the case. Rather than following such mistaken minds, therefore, we should regard all living beings as our mothers. Whoever we meet, we should think 'This person is my mother.' In this way we will feel equally warm towards all living beings.

If we regard all living beings as our mothers we will find it easy to develop pure love and compassion, our everyday relationships will become pure and stable, and we will naturally avoid negative actions such as killing or harming living beings. Since it is so beneficial to regard all living beings as our mothers, we should adopt this way of thinking without hesitation.

Once we have become convinced that all living beings are our mothers we should then contemplate their kindness. When we were conceived, had our mother not wanted to keep us in her womb she could have had an abortion. If she had done so we would not now have this human life. Through her kindness she allowed us to stay in her womb, and so we now enjoy a human life and experience all its advantages. When we were a baby, had we not received her constant care and attention we would certainly have had an accident and could now be handicapped, crippled, or blind. Fortunately our mother did not neglect us. Day and night she gave us her loving care, regarding us as more important than herself. She saved our life many times each day. During the night she allowed her sleep to be interrupted, and during the day she forfeited her usual pleasures. She had to leave her job, and when her friends went out to enjoy themselves she had to stay behind. She spent all her money on us, giving us the best food and the best clothes she could afford. She taught us how to eat, how to walk, how to talk. Thinking of our future welfare, she did her best to ensure that we received a good education. Due to her kindness we are now able to study whatever we choose. It is principally through the kindness of our mother that we now have the opportunity to practise Dharma and eventually to attain enlightenment.

Since there is no one who has not been our mother at some time in our previous lives, and since when we were their child they treated us with the same kindness as our present mother has treated us in this life, all living beings are very kind.

The kindness of living beings is not limited to the times when they have been our mother. All the time, our day-to-day needs are provided through the kindness of others. We brought nothing with us from our former life, yet as soon as we were born we were given a home, food, clothes, and everything we needed – all provided through the kindness of others. Everything we now enjoy has been provided through the generosity of other beings, past or present.

We are able to make use of many things with very little effort on our own part. If we consider facilities such as roads, cars, trains, aeroplanes, ships, restaurants, hotels, libraries, hospitals, shops, money, and so on, it is clear that many people worked very hard to provide these things.

Even though we make little or no contribution towards the provision of these facilities, they are all available for us to use. This shows the great kindness of others.

Both our general education and our spiritual training are provided by others. All our Dharma realizations, from our very first insights up to our eventual attainment of liberation and enlightenment, will be attained in dependence upon the kindness of others.

Through recognizing that all living beings are our mothers and reflecting on their kindness, we will develop affectionate love equally for all living beings. Once a woman asked the great Tibetan Teacher Geshe Potawa what affectionate love is and he replied 'What do you feel when you see your own son? You are delighted to see him and he appears pleasant to you. If we regard all beings in the same way, feeling close to them and holding them dear, we have developed affectionate love.'

Our own mother may not be very beautiful or wear very elegant clothes, but because we have a good relationship with her, in our eyes she is beautiful. We love her, and if we notice that she is in pain we naturally feel compassion for her. If we have this same tender regard for all other living beings we have affectionate love. With this affectionate love for all living beings it is impossible to become jealous of or angry with others. If we improve our awareness of the kindness of others we will naturally develop this warm heart and tenderness and thereby come to cherish others. Even though others may possess faults we will see their beauty, just as a mother sees the beauty of her children, no matter what they do.

GREAT COMPASSION

Great compassion is a spontaneous wish to release all living beings from the sufferings of samsara. Once we have developed affectionate love for all living beings, if we then contemplate how they are all trapped in samsara, experiencing one problem after another, we will easily develop compassion for them. Previously it was explained how to develop renunciation for samsara by contemplating seven types of suffering, from the sufferings of birth up to the suffering of failing to satisfy our desires. If we now recall these contemplations and apply them to others, we will realize that all living beings are experiencing unbearable suffering. We should contemplate these sufferings of others until a strong feeling of compassion for all living beings arises in our heart. Then we should meditate on this feeling without distraction.

BODHICHITTA

When we have developed great compassion for all living beings we should think:

I want to liberate all living beings from samsara, but how can I do this? As long as I remain in samsara myself I have no power to help them. I cannot even solve all my own problems, let alone the problems of all living beings. Only a Buddha has the power to protect all living beings and bestow upon them uncontaminated happiness. Therefore, to fulfil my wish to liberate all living beings from suffering I will become a Buddha.

We meditate on this thought again and again until it arises spontaneously in our mind day and night. When this happens, we have developed the actual realization of bodhichitta and have become a Bodhisattva, a son or daughter of the Buddhas. The mere wish to become a Buddha for the benefit of all living beings is called aspiring bodhichitta. If we then make a heartfelt promise to engage in the Bodhisattva's way of life by practising the six perfections, our aspiring bodhichitta will transform into engaging bodhichitta.

The Bodhisattva's Way of Life

We engage in the Bodhisattva's way of life by practising the six perfections: the perfections of giving, moral discipline, patience, effort, mental stabilization, and wisdom. These are the actual path to Buddhahood. If we wish to become enlightened but do not practise the six perfections we are like someone who wants to go somewhere but does not actually set out on the journey. Bodhisattvas have two main tasks: to benefit others right now and to attain full enlightenment to be able to benefit all living beings in the future. Both tasks are accomplished through the practice of the six perfections. The six perfections will now be explained in detail.

THE PERFECTION OF GIVING

Giving is a virtuous mental intention to give, or a bodily or verbal action of giving that is motivated by a virtuous state of mind. Giving practised with bodhichitta motivation is a perfection of giving. There are three types of giving:

1 Giving material things
2 Giving Dharma
3 Giving fearlessness

Giving material things

To practise giving material things, we first contemplate the disadvantages of miserliness and the benefits of giving,

Buddha Glorious Wealth

*Buddha Glorious
Mindfulness*

*Buddha Glorious Name
of Great Renown*

and then we engage in the actual practice of giving to others. In the *Condensed Perfection of Wisdom Sutra*, Buddha taught that miserliness leads to poverty and rebirth as a hungry ghost. Even in this life, miserliness causes us suffering. It is a tight, uncomfortable mind that leads to isolation and unpopularity. Giving, on the other hand, is a joyful mind that leads us to experience wealth and abundant resources in the future.

There is no point in clinging to our possessions, for wealth acquires meaning only when it is given away or used to benefit others. Since without any choice we shall have to part with all our possessions when we die, it is better to part with them now and thereby derive some benefit from having owned them. Moreover, if at the time of our death we have strong attachment to our possessions, this will prevent us from having a peaceful death and may even prevent us from taking a fortunate rebirth.

When we go on holiday we take care to carry enough money to see us through the whole holiday, but how much more important it is to ensure that we travel to future lives with enough virtue, or merit, to provide us with all the resources we will need. Our practice of giving is the best insurance against future poverty.

We should give away our possessions only when the time is right, that is, when it would not cause any hindrances to our spiritual practice or endanger our life, and when the person to whom we are giving will derive great benefit. Otherwise we should not give away our possessions even if someone asks for them. For example, if we can see that a gift will cause harm to others we should not offer it. We need to consider all the implications of our action, including how it will affect others besides the person who is to receive the gift. We also need to keep those things that are necessary for our Dharma practice. If we were to give these away we would be indirectly harming others because we would be creating obstacles to our progress towards enlightenment for their sake.

We should mentally dedicate all our possessions to others, but we should physically give them away only when it is most suitable to do so. This skilful way of thinking is in itself a form of giving. For example, charitable organisations do not immediately give away everything that is donated to them, but keep a certain amount in reserve for when it is most needed. Even so, while they are holding on to the money they do not consider it to be their own; they simply think that they are looking after it for others until a need arises. If we view all our possessions in a similar way we shall be practising giving all the time.

The amount of merit we accumulate by the practice of giving depends upon several factors besides the actual value of the gift. One factor is the nature of the recipient. There are three classes of being to whom it is especially meritorious to give: holy beings, such as our Spiritual Guide, Buddhas, and Bodhisattvas; those who have shown us great kindness, such as our parents; and those who are in great need, such as the poor, the sick, and the handicapped. Another important factor is our motivation. It is more meritorious to put a few crumbs on a bird table with a motivation of pure compassion than it is to give a diamond ring out of attachment. The best motivation, of course, is bodhichitta. The virtue created by giving with this motivation is limitless.

Giving Dharma

There are many ways to give Dharma. If with a good motivation we teach even just one word of Dharma to others, we are giving Dharma. This is much more beneficial than any kind of material gift because material things help others only in this life, whereas the gift of Dharma helps them in this and all their future lives.

There are many other ways in which we can give Dharma, for example, by dedicating our virtue so that all living beings may enjoy peace and happiness, or by whispering mantras into the ears of animals.

Giving fearlessness

To give fearlessness is to protect other living beings from fear or danger. For example, if we rescue someone from a fire or from some other natural disaster, if we protect others from physical violence, or if we save animals who have fallen into water or who are trapped, we are practising giving fearlessness. If we are not able to rescue those in danger, we can still give fearlessness by making prayers and offerings so that they may be released from danger. We can also practise giving fearlessness by praying for others to become free from their delusions, especially the delusion of self-grasping, which is the ultimate source of all fear.

THE PERFECTION OF MORAL DISCIPLINE

Moral discipline is a virtuous mental determination to abandon any fault, or it is a bodily or verbal action motivated by such a determination. Moral discipline practised with bodhichitta motivation is a perfection of moral discipline. There are three types of moral discipline:

1 The moral discipline of restraint
2 The moral discipline of gathering virtuous Dharmas
3 The moral discipline of benefiting living beings

The moral discipline of restraint

This is the moral discipline of abstaining from non-virtue. To practise this moral discipline we need to understand the dangers of committing negative actions, make a promise or vow to abandon them, and then keep that promise or vow. Simply failing to commit negative actions unintentionally is not a practice of moral discipline because it is not motivated by a determination to abstain.

Any spiritual discipline that avoids or overcomes either mental faults or negative actions of body or speech is included within the moral discipline of restraint. For example, if we understand the dangers of the ten non-virtuous actions, promise to refrain from them, and keep that promise, we are practising the moral discipline of restraint.

Sometimes we can take vows by ourself by recognizing the faults of the actions we want to abandon and promising to refrain from them for whatever length of time we can. Even if we promise to refrain from just one negative action for only a short time – for example if we promise only to abandon killing for just one week – and we keep that promise, we are practising the moral discipline of restraint. However, as our capacity increases we should gradually extend the duration of our restraint, and also promise to abandon other non-virtuous actions. When we feel we are ready, we can take special vows from a Spiritual Guide, such as refuge vows, ordination vows, Bodhisattva vows, and Tantric vows. The refuge vows, or commitments, are explained in Appendix I of this book, and the Bodhisattva vows are explained in *The Bodhisattva Vow*.

To practise moral discipline we need to rely upon mindfulness, alertness, and conscientiousness. Mindfulness prevents us from forgetting our vows, alertness keeps a check on our mind and warns us if delusions are about to arise, and conscientiousness protects our mind from non-virtue. For example, we may be in a situation, such as a lively party, in which it would be easy to incur the Bodhisattva downfall of praising ourself and scorning others. However, if we practise mindfulness we will constantly remember that we have promised not to do such things and there will be no danger of our incurring this downfall out of forgetfulness. Similarly, if we maintain alertness we will be able to detect delusions such as pride or envy as soon as they begin to arise and then use conscientiousness to check their development.

When we take the Bodhisattva vows we must have the intention to keep them continuously until we are enlightened. If we are to fulfil our wish to attain enlightenment quickly for the sake of others, we need to overcome our faults as soon as we can. For a Bodhisattva the main object to be abandoned is the intention to work solely for one's own sake. Bodhisattvas see clearly the dangers of self-cherishing, thinking oneself to be supremely important, and they realize that it is the principal obstacle to developing bodhichitta and to attaining enlightenment. In the *Condensed Perfection of Wisdom Sutra*, Buddha says that the moral discipline of a Bodhisattva does not degenerate if he enjoys beautiful forms, sounds, tastes, or other objects of the senses, but if a Bodhisattva develops concern for his own welfare, both his moral discipline and his bodhichitta degenerate. If we generate bodhichitta and later think that it would be better to seek only our own liberation, we incur a root Bodhisattva downfall and break our moral discipline of restraint.

With the motivation of bodhichitta no action can be non-virtuous because bodhichitta eliminates self-cherishing, which is the root of all non-virtuous actions. Even if a Bodhisattva has to kill, this action is not non-virtuous because it is performed solely for the benefit of all living beings. Although others may condemn them, Bodhisattvas incur no negative karma when they perform such actions because their bodhichitta ensures that all their actions are pure. This is illustrated by an episode from a previous life of Buddha Shakyamuni, while he was still a Bodhisattva. At that time he was the captain of a ship that was ferrying five hundred merchants on a special voyage. With his clairvoyance he saw that one of the merchants was planning to kill all the others. Seeing that as a result of this the merchant would be reborn in hell, he generated great compassion for him and for his intended victims. He decided to take upon himself the karma of killing rather than allow all five hundred merchants to suffer and so, with pure bodhichitta motivation, he killed the wicked merchant. In this way he protected that merchant from a hellish rebirth and saved the lives of all the others. As a result of this action of killing, that Bodhisattva made great spiritual progress.

The moral discipline of gathering virtuous Dharmas

We practise this moral discipline when we sincerely practise any virtuous action, such as keeping the Bodhisattva vows purely, practising the six perfections, making offerings to the Three Jewels, or putting energy into studying, meditating on, or propagating the holy Dharma.

The moral discipline of benefiting living beings

This is the moral discipline of helping others in whatever way we can. If we cannot offer practical help to someone, we can at least make prayers for them and maintain a continuous intention to give assistance when an opportunity arises. We can understand how to practise this moral discipline by studying the instructions on the last eleven secondary downfalls of the Bodhisattva vows, which are explained in *The Bodhisattva Vow*.

When we help others we should be tactful and sensitive. We should try to understand the other person's experience and point of view, and then offer help that is relevant to them, and in such a way that they can accept it. We cannot help others if we attack their values and beliefs, or if we ignore their temperament and their personal circumstances. We have to adapt our own behaviour so that it suits the other person and makes them feel at ease. Instead of imposing our own moral standards on others and passing judgment on them if they do not comply, we should simply act in the way that will have the most positive effect. We need both flexibility of mind and flexibility of behaviour.

Since Bodhisattvas have great compassion they do whatever is necessary to help others. In effect, Bodhisattvas will do whatever needs to be done to make someone else happy because when others are happy their minds are more open and receptive to advice and example. If we wish to influence others we can do so only if we do not antagonize them or make them feel uncomfortable or frightened.

The tact and sensitivity required by a Bodhisattva when helping others is well illustrated by an episode from the life of the great Tibetan Teacher Geshe Langri Tangpa. A woman who had recently given birth to a baby girl was frightened she would lose her baby because she had already given birth to one child who had died in infancy. The woman expressed her anxiety to her mother who told her that children given into the care of Geshe Langri Tangpa would not die. Later, when the little girl fell ill, the woman took her to see Geshe Langri Tangpa, but when she arrived she found him sitting on a throne giving a discourse to a thousand disciples. The woman began to worry that her child would die before the end of the discourse. She knew that Geshe Langri Tangpa was a Bodhisattva and would show patience, and so she walked up to the throne and, in a loud, affronted tone of voice, declared 'Here, take your baby. Now you look after her!' She turned to the audience and said 'This is the father of my child', and then turned back to Geshe Langri

Tangpa and pleaded softly 'Please don't let her die.' Geshe Langri Tangpa just nodded his head in acceptance. As if he really were the father of the child, he wrapped it tenderly in his robes and continued his discourse. His disciples were astonished and asked him 'Are you really the father of that child?' Knowing that if he were to deny it, the woman would have been thought crazy and the people would have ridiculed her, Geshe Langri Tangpa replied that he was.

Although he was a monk, Geshe Langri Tangpa acted like a real father for the child, delighting in her and caring for her. After some time, the mother returned to see if her daughter was well. When she saw how healthy the child was she asked Geshe Langri Tangpa if she could have her back again. The Geshe then kindly returned the girl to her mother. When his disciples realized what had happened they said 'So you are not really the father after all!' and Geshe Langri Tangpa replied 'No, I am not.' In this way, Geshe Langri Tangpa responded to the woman's actions with pure compassion and acted in accordance with the needs of the time.

THE PERFECTION OF PATIENCE

Patience is a virtuous mind that is able to bear harm, suffering, or profound Dharma. Patience practised with bodhichitta motivation is a perfection of patience.

We need to cultivate patience even if we have no interest in spiritual development because without it we remain vulnerable to anxiety, frustration, and disquiet. If we lack patience it is difficult for us to maintain peaceful relationships with others.

Patience is the opponent to anger, the most potent destroyer of virtue. We can see from our own experience how much suffering arises from anger. It prevents us from judging a situation correctly and it causes us to act in regrettable ways. It destroys our own peace of mind and disturbs everyone else we meet. Even people who are normally attracted to us are repelled when they see us angry. Anger can make us reject or insult our own parents, and when it is intense it can even drive us to kill the people we love, or even to take our own life.

Usually anger is triggered off by something quite insignificant, such as a comment that we take personally, a habit that we find irritating, or an expectation that was not fulfilled. Based on such small experiences, anger weaves an elaborate fantasy, exaggerating the unpleasantness of the situation, and providing rationalizations and justifications for the sense of disappointment, outrage, or resentment. It leads us to say and do harmful things, thereby causing offence to others and transforming a small difficulty into a great problem.

If we were asked 'Who caused all the wars in which so many people have died?', we would have to reply that they were caused by angry minds. If nations were full of calm, peace-loving people, how could wars ever arise? Anger is the greatest enemy of living beings. It harmed us in the past, it harms us now, and, if we do not overcome it through the practice of patience, it will continue to harm us in the future. As Shantideva says:

This enemy of anger has no function
Other than to cause me harm.

External enemies harm us in slower and less subtle ways, and if we practise patience with them we can even win them over and turn them into our friends, but there can be no reconciliation with anger. If we are lenient with anger it will take advantage of us and harm us even more. Moreover, whereas external enemies can harm us only in this life, anger harms us for many future lives. Therefore, we need to eliminate anger as soon as it enters our mind because if we do not it will quickly become a blazing fire that consumes our merit.

Buddha King of the Victory Banner

*Buddha Glorious One
Complete Subduer*

*Buddha Great
Victor in Battle*

Patience, on the other hand, helps us in this life and in all future lives. Shantideva says:

There is no evil like anger
And no virtue like patience.

With patience, we can accept any pain that is inflicted upon us and we can easily endure our usual troubles and indispositions. With patience, nothing upsets our peace of mind and we do not experience problems. With patience, we maintain an inner peace and tranquillity that allows spiritual realizations to grow. Chandrakirti says that if we practise patience we will have a beautiful form in the future, and we will become a holy being with high realizations.

There are three types of patience:

1 The patience of not retaliating
2 The patience of voluntarily enduring suffering
3 The patience of definitely thinking about Dharma

The patience of not retaliating

To practise this type of patience we need to remain continuously mindful of the dangers of anger and the benefits of patient acceptance, and whenever anger is about to arise we need immediately to apply the methods for eliminating it. We have to begin by learning to forbear small difficulties such as insignificant insults or minor disruptions in our routine, and then gradually to improve our patience until we are able to forbear even the greatest difficulty without getting angry.

When we are meditating on patience we can use many different lines of reasoning to help us overcome our tendency to retaliate. For example, we can contemplate that if someone were to hit us with a stick we would not get angry with the stick because it was being wielded by the attacker and had no choice. In the same way, if someone insults us or harms us, we should not get angry with them because they are being manipulated by their deluded minds and also have no choice. Similarly, we can think that just as a doctor does not get angry if a feverish patient lashes out at him, so we should not get angry if confused living beings suffering from the sickness of the delusions harm us in any way. There are many special lines of reasoning such as these to be found in *Joyful Path of Good Fortune* and *Meaningful to Behold*.

The fundamental reason why we receive harm is that we have harmed others in the past. Those who attack us are merely the conditions whereby our karma ripens; the real cause of all the harm we receive is our own negativity. If in such circumstances we retaliate, we simply create more negative karma and so we will have to suffer even more harm in the future. By patiently accepting injury, however, the chain is broken and that particular karmic debt is paid off.

The patience of voluntarily enduring suffering

If we do not have the patience of voluntarily enduring suffering we become discouraged whenever we encounter obstacles and whenever our wishes go unfulfilled. We find it hard to complete our tasks because we feel like abandoning them as soon as they become difficult, and our miseries are further aggravated by our impatience. However, it is possible to accept and endure pain if we have a good reason to do so, and whenever we practise such patience we actually reduce our sufferings. For example, if someone were to stick a sharp needle into our flesh we would find the pain unbearable, but if the needle contained a vaccine that we needed, our tolerance would increase considerably.

Even to succeed in worldly aims people are prepared to endure adversity. Businessmen sacrifice their leisure and peace of mind just to make money, and soldiers put up with extreme hardship simply to kill other soldiers. How much more willing should we be to bear difficulties for the sake of the most worthwhile aim of all – the attainment of enlightenment for the benefit of all living beings? Because we are in samsara we often have to endure unpleasant conditions and misfortune. With the patience of voluntarily enduring suffering, however, we can happily and courageously accept these adversities whenever they arise. When our wishes are not fulfilled, or when we are sick, bereaved, or otherwise in difficulty, we should not be discouraged. Instead of feeling self-pity, we should use our suffering to strengthen our spiritual practice. We can recall that all our suffering is the result of our previous negative karma and resolve to practise pure moral discipline in the future; or we can contemplate that for as long as we remain in samsara suffering is inevitable, and thereby increase our wish to escape from samsara; or we can use our own suffering as an illustration of the much greater suffering experienced by other beings and in this way strengthen our compassion.

If we are able to endure adversities we will reap great rewards. Our present sufferings will diminish and we will accomplish both our temporary and our ultimate wishes. Thus, suffering should not be seen as an obstacle to our spiritual practice but as an indispensable aid. As Shantideva says:

Moreover, suffering has good qualities.
Because of sorrow, pride is dispelled,
Compassion arises for those trapped in samsara,
Evil is shunned, and joy is found in virtue.

The patience of definitely thinking about Dharma

If we listen to, contemplate, or meditate on Dharma with a patient and joyful mind so as to gain a special experience of it, we are practising the patience of definitely thinking about Dharma. Such patience is important because if our mind is impatient or unhappy when we engage in Dharma practice, this will obstruct our spiritual progress and prevent us from improving our Dharma wisdom. Even if we find some aspects of our Dharma practice difficult we still need to engage in them with a happy mind.

THE PERFECTION OF EFFORT

Effort is a mind that delights in virtue. Effort practised with bodhichitta motivation is a perfection of effort. Effort is not something to be practised separately, but a practice that should accompany all our virtuous endeavours. We practise effort when we apply ourself enthusiastically to Dharma study or meditation, strive to accomplish Dharma realizations, or put effort into helping others. Applying ourself energetically to non-virtuous or neutral actions, however, is not a practice of effort.

With effort we can attain mundane and supramundane happiness – it enables us to complete those virtuous actions that cause birth in the fortunate realms as well as those that lead to liberation and enlightenment. With effort we can purify all our negativities and attain whatever good qualities we wish for. However, without effort, even if our wisdom is sharp we will be unable to complete our spiritual practices.

To generate effort we need to overcome the three types of laziness: procrastination, attraction to what is meaningless or non-virtuous, and discouragement. Procrastination is a reluctance or unwillingness to put effort into spiritual practice immediately. For example, although we may have an interest in Dharma and intend to practise it, we may feel that we can postpone our practice until some point in the future, when we have had a holiday, when the children have grown up, or when we retire. This is a dangerous attitude because the opportunity to practise Dharma is easily lost. Death can strike at any time. Moreover, when we have finished the particular task that is presently preventing us from practising Dharma, we can be certain that another will arise to take its place. Worldly activities are like an old man's beard – though he may shave it off in the morning, it has grown again by the evening. Therefore, we should abandon procrastination and begin to practise Dharma immediately. The best remedy for the laziness of procrastination is to meditate on our precious human life and on death and impermanence.

Most of us are very familiar with the second type of laziness. We give in to it whenever we watch television for hours on end without caring what comes on, when we indulge in prolonged conversations with no purpose, or when we become engrossed in sports or business ventures for their own sake. Activities such as these dissipate the energy we have for practising Dharma. Though they may seem pleasant they deceive us, wasting our precious human life and destroying our opportunity to attain real and lasting happiness. To overcome this type of laziness we need to meditate again and again on the dangers of samsara, remembering that all the entertainments of worldly life are deceptive because in reality they serve only to bind us within samsara and cause us even more suffering.

The laziness of discouragement is very common in these degenerate times. Since we cannot see with our own eyes living examples of enlightened beings, and since our spiritual progress is often much slower than we expect it to be, we may begin to doubt whether Buddhahood is possible, or we may conclude that it must be so rare that there is almost no hope of attaining it. We may also see faults in our Spiritual Guide and in those who are practising Dharma and conclude that they have no realizations, and that effort put into Dharma practice is wasted. If we find we are becoming discouraged in this way we need to remember that every appearance to the minds of ordinary beings is mistaken because it is contaminated by ignorance. However, we can be certain that when through practising Dharma sincerely we eliminate our ignorance and attain pure minds, pure beings such as Buddhas will definitely appear clearly to us.

If we strive to attain higher realizations before we have mastered the basics, we must expect to become discouraged. We need to understand that even the highest realizations have small beginnings, and learn to value the small experiences of Dharma that we have already attained. Perhaps our attitude towards other people is less biased than it used to be, perhaps we are more patient or less arrogant, or perhaps our faith is stronger. These small improvements are the seeds that will eventually grow into higher realizations, and we should cherish them accordingly. We should not expect great changes straight away. We all have Buddha nature, the potential to attain great enlightenment, and now that we have met perfect instructions on the Mahayana path, if we practise steadily without becoming discouraged, eventually we will definitely attain enlightenment without having to undergo great hardships. So what reason is there to become discouraged?

There are three types of effort: armour-like effort, which is a strong determination to succeed that we generate at the beginning of a virtuous action; the effort of gathering virtuous Dharmas, which is the actual effort we apply when we strive to gain Dharma realizations; and the effort of benefiting others, which is the effort we apply when we strive to benefit other living beings.

We need to apply effort in a skilful way. Some people begin their practice with great enthusiasm and then give up when great results do not appear, like a waterfall caused by a sudden storm cascading furiously for a short time and then trickling away to nothing. Our effort should not be like this. At the very beginning of our practice we should make a firm decision that we will persevere until we attain Buddhahood no matter how long it takes, even if it takes many lives. Then we should practise gently and consistently, like a great river that flows day and night, year after year.

When we are tired we should relax, and resume our effort when we are properly rested. If we try to force ourself beyond our natural capacity we will only become tense, irritable, or sick. Dharma practice should be a joyful affair. It is said that when we practise Dharma we should be like a child at play. When children are engrossed in their games they feel completely contented and nothing can distract them.

THE PERFECTION OF MENTAL STABILIZATION

Mental stabilization, or concentration, is a mind whose nature is to be single-pointedly placed on a virtuous object and whose function is to prevent distraction. Any concentration practised with bodhichitta motivation is a perfection of mental stabilization.

For ordinary beings, concentration functions mainly by means of mental awareness. Our sense awarenesses can behold and remain single-pointedly on their objects, but these are not concentrations. For example, when our eye awareness stares single-pointedly at a candle, or our ear awareness becomes absorbed in a piece of music, we are not practising concentration. To improve our concentration so that we attain the nine mental abidings and eventually tranquil abiding, it is necessary for our mind to gather within and dwell upon its object single-pointedly. To accomplish this, we must take as our main object of concentration a generic image, or mental image, that appears to the mental awareness. Eventually, through the power of concentration, the generic image is worn away and the object is perceived directly.

There are many benefits from training in concentration. When the mind is stilled by concentration, the delusions subside and the mind becomes extremely lucid. At the moment our minds are intractable, refusing to cooperate with our virtuous intentions; but concentration melts the tension in our body and mind and makes them supple, comfortable, and easy to work with. It is difficult for a distracted mind to become sufficiently acquainted with its object to induce spontaneous realizations because it feels as if the mind is 'here' and the object 'there'. A concentrated mind, however, enters into its object and mixes with it and, as a result, realizations of the stages of the path are quickly attained.

Mental stabilization can be used for either mundane or supramundane purposes. The highest planes within samsara are entered by refining the mind through the practice of concentration. Samsara has three levels: the desire realm, the form realm, and the formless realm. The three lower realms, the human realm, the demi-god realm, and the lowest level of the god realm are all included within the desire realm. The god realm is divided into three levels: the realm of the desire realm gods, the realm of the form realm gods, and the realm of the formless realm gods. The only way to attain rebirth as a form realm god or a formless realm god is to train in mental stabilization.

Once a meditator has attained tranquil abiding he can, if he wishes, go on to attain rebirth in the form and formless realms. He begins by contemplating the gross and painful nature of the desire realm and the relative peace, purity, and subtlety of the form realm. Gradually he abandons the delusions pertaining to the desire realm – principally sensual desire and all forms of anger – so that in his next life he can be reborn as a god of the form realm. If the meditator continues to refine his mind he will gradually ascend to progressively more and more subtle levels of concentration until eventually he attains the concentration of the peak of samsara. With this concentration, he can be reborn in the peak of samsara, the highest level of the formless realm, and the highest attainment within samsara. Such a rebirth is attained mainly through the force of concentration, without the wisdom realizing emptiness. Some non-Buddhists mistakenly believe this to be a state of liberation but, although at this stage gross delusions have been suppressed, very subtle delusions still have not been eliminated and so eventually the grosser delusions will arise and once again the meditator will have to descend to lower states. Only a direct realization of emptiness has the power to cut the continuum of self-grasping, the root of all delusions, and thereby release us from samsara altogether. Therefore, from the beginning we should train in tranquil abiding with the motivation of renunciation and bodhichitta so that we can overcome self-grasping together with its imprints and attain great liberation.

In earlier times it was fairly easy to attain tranquil abiding and the form realm and formless realm absorptions, but nowadays, as our merit decreases, our delusions grow stronger, and distractions abound, these attainments are much more difficult. Therefore we need to prepare well, especially by overcoming desirous attachment, and then be willing to practise steadily for a long time before we can attain higher levels of concentration.

In the course of mastering the concentrations of the form and formless realms we attain clairvoyance and other miracle powers. Although these have little meaning in themselves, they can be used by Bodhisattvas to enhance their ability to help others. For example, although we may have very good intentions, sometimes, through not knowing others' minds, we misjudge a situation and our actions prove to be more of a hindrance than a help. Such problems can be overcome by developing a clairvoyance that knows others' minds. However, we should not strive to attain clairvoyance and miracle powers simply for our own sake. If we have taken Bodhisattva vows, we should have a strong interest in improving our concentration only as a means of fulfilling our wish to benefit others.

THE PERFECTION OF WISDOM

Wisdom is a virtuous mind that functions mainly to dispel doubt and confusion by understanding its object thoroughly. Wisdom that is motivated by bodhichitta is a perfection of wisdom.

Wisdom is not the same as worldly intelligence. It is possible to have great intelligence but little wisdom. For example, people who invent weapons of mass destruction are very clever from a worldly point of view, but they have very little wisdom. Similarly, there are people who know a great many facts and understand complex technical subjects, but have no idea how to maintain a peaceful mind and lead a virtuous life. Such people may have great intelligence, but they have little wisdom.

Wisdom is a special type of understanding that induces peace of mind by clearly distinguishing what is virtuous and to be practised from what is non-virtuous and to be avoided. Wisdom provides our spiritual practice with vision. Without the guidance of wisdom the other five perfections would be blind and would not be able to lead us to the final destination of Buddhahood.

A direct realization of ultimate truth, emptiness, can be attained only by a wisdom that is conjoined with tranquil abiding. With a wavering mind we will never perceive a subtle object such as emptiness clearly enough to be able to realize it directly, just as we cannot read a book properly by the light of a flickering candle. Training in mental stabilization is like shielding our mind from the winds of distracting thoughts, while wisdom is like the light of the flame itself. When these two factors are brought together we attain a clear and powerful perception of the object.

After attaining tranquil abiding we should strive to attain a union of tranquil abiding and superior seeing observing emptiness. The nature of superior seeing is wisdom. Just as tranquil abiding is a special and superior kind of concentration, so superior seeing is a superior wisdom arising in dependence upon tranquil abiding. When we have attained tranquil abiding our concentration cannot be disturbed by conceptual thoughts. It is unshakeable like a huge mountain that cannot be moved by the wind. With such stable concentration we can investigate our observed object more thoroughly. Through the power of repeated investigation, eventually we will gain a superior knowledge of, or insight into, the nature of our object of meditation. This wisdom of investigation induces a special mental suppleness. A wisdom that is qualified by such suppleness is superior seeing.

The principal object of superior seeing is emptiness, the ultimate nature of phenomena. Every phenomenon has two natures: a conventional nature and an ultimate nature. Our mind, for example, has various characteristics and functions, such as its clarity and its ability to cognize objects. These are the conventional nature of the mind. Although the mind has these uncommon characteristics which distinguish it from other phenomena, it does not exist from its own side, independent of other objects. The mind's lack of existing from its own side is its ultimate nature, or emptiness. Emptiness will be explained in more detail in the next chapter.

When we first attain superior seeing observing emptiness our realization of emptiness is still conceptual, but by continuing to meditate on emptiness with the union of tranquil abiding and superior seeing we can gradually eliminate the generic image until finally we perceive emptiness directly, without even a trace of conceptuality. A wisdom that realizes emptiness directly has the power to eradicate delusions from the mind, therefore it is a true path that leads to liberation and enlightenment.

Since Bodhisattvas wish to become enlightened as quickly as possible they have a strong wish to accumulate powerful merit quickly, therefore they practise each of the six perfections in conjunction with all the others. For example, when Bodhisattvas practise giving they do so without self-interest, expecting nothing in return. In this way they practise in accordance with their Bodhisattva vows and combine the perfection of giving with the perfection of moral discipline. By patiently accepting any hardships involved and not allowing anger to arise if no gratitude is shown, they combine the perfection of giving with the perfection of patience. By giving joyfully they combine the perfection of giving with the perfection of effort; and by concentrating their minds, thinking 'May the merit of my action of giving enable this person to attain Buddhahood', they combine it with the perfection of mental stabilization. Finally, by realizing that the giver, the gift, and the action of giving all lack inherent existence, they combine the perfection of giving with the perfection of wisdom.

The other perfections can also be practised in this way, with each perfection being practised in conjunction with all the others. This is the armour-like skilful action of a Bodhisattva that hastens the completion of the two collections – the collection of merit and the collection of wisdom – that are the causes of the Form Body and the

Truth Body of a Buddha respectively. Because Bodhisattvas perform all their actions with the motivation of bodhichitta their whole life is taken up with the practice of the six perfections.

Buddha Glorious One Complete
Subduer Passed Beyond

Buddha Glorious Array
Illuminating All

Buddha Jewel Lotus
Great Subduer

Ultimate Truth

Ultimate truth is emptiness. Emptiness is not nothingness, but lack of inherent existence. Inherent existence is mistakenly projected onto phenomena by our self-grasping mind. All phenomena naturally appear to our mind to be inherently existent and, without realizing that this appearance is mistaken, we instinctively assent to it and hold phenomena to exist inherently, or truly. This is the fundamental reason why we are in samsara.

There are two stages to realizing emptiness. The first is clearly to identify the way phenomena appear to our mind to be inherently existent, and how we firmly believe in the truth of this appearance. This is called 'identifying the object of negation'. If our understanding of emptiness is to be effective it is essential that we begin with a very clear image of what is to be negated. The second stage is to refute the object of negation, that is, to prove to ourself using various lines of reasoning that the object of negation does not actually exist. In this way we will come to realize the absence, or non-existence, of the object of negation, which is emptiness.

Because we grasp most strongly at ourself and our body, we should begin by contemplating the emptiness of these two phenomena. We can do this by training in the two meditations explained below: meditation on the emptiness of the I and meditation on the emptiness of the body.

THE EMPTINESS OF THE I

Identifying the object of negation

Although we grasp at an inherently existent I all the time, even during sleep, it is not easy to identify how it appears to our mind. To identify it clearly we must begin by allowing it to manifest strongly by contemplating situations in which we have an exaggerated sense of I, such as when we are embarrassed, ashamed, afraid, or indignant. We recall or imagine such a situation and then, without any comment or analysis, try to attain a clear mental image of how the I naturally appears at such times. We have to be patient at this stage because it may take many sessions before we attain a clear image. Eventually we shall see that the I appears to be completely solid and real, existing from its own side without depending upon the body or the mind. This vividly appearing I is the inherently existent I that we cherish so strongly. It is the I that we defend when we are criticized, and that we are so proud of when we are praised.

Once we have an image of how the I appears in these extreme circumstances, we should try to identify how it appears normally, in less extreme situations. For example, we can observe the I that is presently reading this book and try to discover how it appears to our mind. Eventually we shall see that, although in this case there is not such an inflated sense of I, nevertheless the I still appears to be inherently existent, existing from its own side without depending upon the body or the mind.

Once we have an image of the inherently existent I, we focus on it for a while with single-pointed concentration, and then we proceed to the second stage.

Refuting the object of negation

If the I exists in the way that it appears, it must exist in one of four ways: as the body, as the mind, as the collection of the body and mind, or as something separate from the body and mind; there is no other possibility. We contemplate this carefully until we become convinced that this is the case and then we proceed to examine each of the four possibilities:

1 If the I is the body, there is no sense in saying 'my body', because the possessor and the possessed are identical.

   If the I is the body, there is no rebirth because the I ceases when the body dies.

   If the I and the body are identical, then since we are capable of developing faith, dreaming, solving mathematical puzzles, and so on, it follows that flesh, blood, and bones can do the same.

   Since none of this is true, it follows that the I is not the body.

2 If the I is the mind, there is no sense in saying 'my mind', because the possessor and the possessed are identical, but usually when we focus on our mind we say 'my mind'. This clearly indicates that the I is not the mind.

   If the I is the mind, then since each person has many types of mind, such as the six consciousnesses, conceptual minds, and non-conceptual minds, it follows that each person has just as many I's. Since this is absurd, it follows that the I is not the mind.

3 Since the body is not the I and the mind is not the I, the collection of the body and mind cannot be the I. The collection of the body and mind is a collection of things that are not the I, so how can the collection itself be the I? For example, in a herd of cows none of the animals is a sheep, therefore the herd itself is not sheep. In the same way, in the collection of the body and mind, neither the body

nor the mind is the I, therefore the collection itself is not the I.

You may find this point difficult to understand but if you think about it for a long time, with a calm and positive mind, and discuss it with more experienced practitioners, it will gradually become clear to you. You can also consult authentic books on the subject such as *Heart of Wisdom*.

4 If the I is not the body, not the mind, and not the collection of the body and mind, the only possibility that remains is that it is something separate from the body and mind. If this is the case, we must be able to apprehend the I without either the body or the mind appearing, but if we imagine that our body and our mind were completely to disappear there would be nothing remaining that could be called the I. Therefore it follows that the I is not separate from the body and mind.

We should imagine that our body gradually dissolves into thin air. Then our mind dissolves, our thoughts scatter with the wind, our feelings, wishes, and awareness melt into nothingness. Is there anything left that is the I? There is nothing. Clearly the I is not something separate from the body and mind.

We have now examined all four possibilities and have failed to find the I. Since we have already decided that there is no fifth possibility, we must conclude that the truly existent, or inherently existent I that normally appears so vividly does not exist at all. Where there previously appeared an inherently existent I, there now appears an absence of that I. This absence of an inherently existent I is emptiness, ultimate truth.

We contemplate in this way until there appears to our mind a generic image of the absence of an inherently

existent I. This image is our object of placement meditation. We try to become completely familiar with it by
concentrating on it single-pointedly.

Because we have grasped at an inherently existent I
since beginningless time, and have cherished it more
dearly than anything else, the experience of failing to find
the I in meditation can be quite shocking at first. Some
people develop fear, thinking that they have become
completely non-existent. Others feel great joy, as if the
source of all their problems is vanishing. Both reactions
are good signs and indicate correct meditation. After a
while, these initial reactions will subside and our mind
will settle into a more balanced state. Then we will be
able to meditate on emptiness in a calm, controlled man-
ner. We should allow our mind to become absorbed in
space-like emptiness for as long as possible. It is important to remember that our object is emptiness, the absence
of an inherently existent I, not mere nothingness.
Occasionally we should check our meditation with alertness. If our mind has wandered to another object, or if
we have lost the meaning of emptiness and are focusing
on mere nothingness, we should return to the contemplations to bring emptiness clearly to mind once again.

We may wonder 'If there is no truly existent I, then who
is meditating? Who will get up from meditation, speak to
others, and reply when my name is called?' Though there
is nothing within the body and mind, or separate from
the body and mind, that is the I, this does not mean that
the I does not exist at all. Although the I does not exist
in any of the four ways mentioned above, it does exist
conventionally. The I is merely a designation imputed by
the conceptual mind upon the collection of the body and
mind. So long as we are satisfied with the mere designation 'I', there is no problem. We can think 'I exist', 'I
am going to town', and so on. The problem arises only
when we look for an I other than the mere conceptual

imputation, 'I'. The self-grasping mind holds to an I that ultimately exists, independent of conceptual imputation, as if there were a 'real' I existing behind the label. If such an I existed we would be able to find it, but we have seen that the I cannot be found upon investigation. The conclusion of our search was a definite non-finding of the I. This unfindability of the I is the emptiness of the I, the ultimate nature of the I. The I that exists as mere imputation is the conventional nature of the I.

THE EMPTINESS OF THE BODY

Identifying the object of negation

The way to meditate on the emptiness of the body is similar to the way we meditate on the emptiness of the I. First we must identify the object of negation.

Normally when we think 'my body', a body that exists from its own side and is a single entity not depending upon its parts, appears to our mind. Such a body is the object of negation and is non-existent. 'Truly existent body', 'inherently existent body', and 'body that exists from its own side', all have the same meaning, and all are objects of negation.

Refuting the object of negation

If the body exists as it appears, it must exist in one of two ways: as its parts or separate from its parts; there is no third possibility.

If the body is one with its parts, is it the individual parts or the collection of its parts? If it is the individual parts, then is it the hands, the face, the skin, the bones, the flesh, or the internal organs? By checking carefully 'Is the head the body? Is the flesh the body?' and so on, we will easily see that none of the individual parts of the body is the body.

If the body is not its individual parts, is it the collection of its parts? The collection of the parts of the body cannot be the body. Why? The parts of the body are all non-bodies, so how can a collection of non-bodies be a body? The hands, feet, and so forth are all parts of the body, but not the body itself. Even though all these parts are assembled together, this collection remains simply parts; it does not magically transform into the part-possessor, the body.

If the body is not its parts, the only other possibility is that it is separate from its parts; but if all the parts of the body were to disappear there would be nothing left that could be called the body. We should imagine that all the parts of our body melt into light and disappear. First the skin dissolves, then the flesh, blood, and internal organs, and finally the skeleton melts and vanishes into light. Is there anything left that is our body? There is nothing. There is no body separate from its parts.

We have now exhausted all possibilities. The body is not its parts and it is not separate from its parts. Clearly, the body cannot be found. Where previously there appeared an inherently existent body, there now appears an absence of that body. This absence of an inherently existent body is the emptiness of the body.

Recognizing this absence to be the lack of an inherently existent body, we meditate on it single-pointedly. Once again, we should examine our meditation with alertness to make sure that we are meditating on the emptiness of the body and not on nothingness. If we lose the meaning of emptiness, we should return to the contemplations to restore it.

As with the I, the fact that the body cannot be found upon investigation does not imply that the body does not exist at all. The body does exist, but only as a conventional imputation. In accordance with accepted convention, we can impute 'body' to the assembly of limbs, trunk, and head; but if we try to pinpoint the body, hoping to find a substantially existent phenomenon to which the word 'body' refers, we find no body. This unfindability of the body is the emptiness of the body, the ultimate nature of the body. The body that exists as mere imputation is the conventional nature of the body.

Although it is incorrect to assert that the body is identical with the collection of the limbs, trunk, and head, there is no fault in saying that the body is imputed upon this collection. Even though the parts of the body are plural, the body is singular. 'Body' is simply an imputation made by the mind that imputes it. It does not exist from the object's side. There is no fault in imputing a singular phenomenon to a group of many things. For example, we can impute the singular 'forest' to a group of many trees, or 'herd' to a group of many cows.

All phenomena exist by way of convention; nothing is inherently existent. This applies to mind, Buddha, and even to emptiness itself. Everything is merely imputed by mind. All phenomena have parts because physical phenomena have physical parts, and non-physical phenomena have various attributes that can be distinguished by thought. Using the same type of reasoning as above, we can realize that any phenomenon is not one of its parts, not the collection of its parts, and not separate from its parts. In this way we can realize the emptiness of all phenomena.

It is particularly helpful to meditate on the emptiness of objects that arouse in us strong delusions such as attachment or anger. By analysing correctly we will realize that the object we desire, or the object we dislike, does not exist from its own side – its beauty or ugliness, and even its very existence, are imputed by mind. By thinking in this way we will discover that there is no basis for attachment or hatred.

Due to our bad mental habits arising through beginningless familiarity with self-grasping ignorance, whatever appears to our mind appears to exist from its own side. This appearance is utterly mistaken. In fact, phenomena are completely empty of existing from their own side. Phenomena exist only through being imputed by mind. By familiarizing ourself with this truth we can eradicate self-grasping, the root of all delusions and faults.

During the day when we are not in meditation we should try to recognize that whatever appears to our mind lacks true existence. In a dream things appear vividly to the dreamer, but when the dreamer wakes he or she immediately realizes that the objects that appeared in the dream were just mental appearances that did not exist from their own side. We should view all phenomena in a similar way. Though they appear vividly to our mind, they lack inherent existence.

Buddha King of Mount Meru

Enlightenment

To attain full enlightenment we need to progress through five stages called the 'five Mahayana paths'. These are:

1 The Mahayana path of accumulation
2 The Mahayana path of preparation
3 The Mahayana path of seeing
4 The Mahayana path of meditation
5 The Mahayana path of No More Learning

They are called 'paths' because just as external paths lead to external destinations, so these internal paths lead us to our ultimate spiritual destination, full enlightenment.

Through training in affectionate love, great compassion, and bodhichitta, eventually we reach the point where we are so familiar with bodhichitta that it arises naturally, day and night. When we attain this spontaneous realization of bodhichitta we become a Bodhisattva and enter the first of the five Mahayana paths, the path of accumulation. Bodhisattvas on the path of accumulation strive to accumulate merit and wisdom by practising the six perfections. During the meditation break they practise mainly the first four perfections to accumulate merit and to benefit others directly. Of the many ways in which Bodhisattvas help others, the most important is by teaching Dharma. By giving Dharma teachings and guiding others along spiritual paths, Bodhisattvas help living beings to attain pure and lasting happiness. This is not something that can be done just by giving material aid.

Towards the end of the path of accumulation, Bodhisattvas attain a special realization called the 'concentration
of the Dharma continuum'. With this concentration they
can remember all the Dharma they have studied and
understood in previous lives, and they never forget anything they learn in this life. They are also able to see
directly the Supreme Emanation Bodies of Buddhas and
to receive teachings from them.

In the meditation session, Bodhisattvas on the path of
accumulation emphasize the perfections of mental
stabilization and wisdom. The main task of a Bodhisattva
on this path is to develop a union of tranquil abiding and
superior seeing observing emptiness. Most Bodhisattvas
on the path of accumulation already have an understanding of emptiness and, since it is impossible to
develop spontaneous bodhichitta without tranquil abiding, they have necessarily attained tranquil abiding. They
now need to combine their understanding of emptiness
with their experience of tranquil abiding through
repeated analytical and placement meditation on emptiness. Eventually they reach the point where, rather than
interfering with the stability of their concentration,
analysis actually enhances their concentration. For them,
the concentration of tranquil abiding is like clear and
still water and the analysis of superior seeing is like a
small fish that swims through the water without disturb-
ing its tranquillity. The moment a Bodhisattva attains
the union of tranquil abiding and superior seeing
observing emptiness he or she advances to the path of
preparation.

The path of preparation is so called because the
Bodhisattva is now preparing for a direct realization of
emptiness. In the meditation break the Bodhisattva
continues to engage in the perfections of giving, moral
discipline, patience, and effort to benefit others and to
accumulate merit, and in the meditation session he or she

continues to meditate on emptiness. At this stage the Bodhisattva's meditation on emptiness is still conceptual, that is, emptiness still appears to his mind mixed with a generic image. Because of this he still has dualistic appearance. The goal of the Mahayana path of preparation is to bring the mind and its object, emptiness, closer and closer together until eventually they mix completely, the generic image dissolves, and all dualistic appearances subside into emptiness. This is attained through repeated meditation on emptiness with a union of tranquil abiding and superior seeing.

To eradicate dualistic appearances, Bodhisattvas meditate on the emptiness of the mind and the emptiness of emptiness. By engaging in these profound meditations with the wisdom of superior seeing, they are able to overcome progressively more and more subtle levels of dualistic appearance. Finally even the most subtle dualistic appearance ceases during meditative equipoise and the mind and emptiness mix like water mixing with water. At this point the mind and its object feel the same. Only emptiness is perceived – no other phenomenon, not even the mind, appears. With this attainment the Bodhisattva becomes a Superior being and advances to the Mahayana path of seeing.

The path of seeing is so called because on this path emptiness is seen directly, without the interference of a generic image. Having seen ultimate truth directly, the Bodhisattva's mind is in perfect accord with reality. Because he or she can no longer be deceived by appearances, the Bodhisattva becomes a perfectly reliable source of refuge, a Sangha Jewel.

On the path of seeing, the Bodhisattva abandons intellectually-formed delusions, which are delusions formed through incorrect reasoning or through adhering to wrong philosophical or religious views. This is because once he has directly seen emptiness, the real nature of phenomena, it is impossible for these delusions ever to arise in his mind again.

At the same time as attaining the Mahayana path of seeing, the Bodhisattva also attains the first of the ten Bodhisattva grounds, called 'Very Joyful'. A Bodhisattva on this ground attains many extraordinary qualities. Strong delusions such as anger and jealousy can no longer arise in his or her mind. For example, no matter how much he is provoked he will never get angry. Moreover, at this stage he does not experience any pain, even if someone were to cut his body piece by piece. Having realized directly that both himself and his body are empty of inherent existence, being merely imputed by conception, he would feel no more pain when his body was cut than he would if he saw a tree being cut. A Bodhisattva on the first ground also possesses special qualities based on the number 'one hundred'. For example, he or she can see a hundred Buddhas in one instant, look a hundred aeons into the past and future, and emanate a hundred bodies simultaneously. These special qualities are explained in *Ocean of Nectar*.

On each of the ten grounds the Bodhisattva attains a special experience of one of the perfections. On the first ground he or she attains a surpassing realization of the perfection of giving. If it benefited living beings, he could give away his body and his life without the slightest regret. On the second ground he attains a surpassing realization of the perfection of moral discipline and does not commit a single negative action, even in his dreams. On the third ground he attains a surpassing realization of the perfection of patience, and on the fourth, fifth, and sixth grounds he attains surpassing realizations of the perfections of effort, mental stabilization, and wisdom respectively. On the seventh, eighth, ninth, and tenth grounds the Bodhisattva attains special experiences of the perfections of skilful means, prayer, power, and exalted wisdom, all of which are aspects of the perfection of wisdom.

Although a Bodhisattva on the path of seeing abandons intellectually-formed delusions, he cannot yet abandon innate delusions. These are the delusions we are born with, as opposed to those we acquire through exposure to incorrect systems of thought, and since they are very deeply ingrained in our mind, they are more difficult to abandon than intellectually-formed delusions.

When his or her meditation on emptiness becomes powerful enough to abandon the grossest level of innate delusions, the Bodhisattva advances to the path of meditation. There are nine levels of innate delusion – from big-big to small-small. Purifying our mind of these delusions is rather like washing dirty clothes. If our clothes are very dirty we need to wash them several times before they become completely clean. The worst dirt comes off in the first wash, but to remove the more subtle and ingrained stains we may have to wash our clothes several times. In the same way, we cannot cleanse our mind of delusions all at once. To purify our mind completely we need to meditate on emptiness again and again. First we abandon the grossest delusions and then we gradually abandon progressively more and more subtle levels of delusion.

On the seventh ground, the Bodhisattva develops a wisdom powerful enough to abandon the subtlest delusions, the small-small delusions; and on the eighth ground he has completely abandoned all delusions, including the small-small delusions. However, the Bodhisattva still has the imprints of the delusions, which remain in his or her mind rather as the smell of garlic remains in a container after the garlic itself has been removed. As mentioned before, the imprints of the delusions are the obstructions to omniscience. The Bodhisattva on the eighth ground meditates on emptiness to abandon gross obstructions to omniscience. When he has abandoned these completely he advances to the ninth ground. On the ninth ground he continues to meditate on emptiness to abandon the subtle obstructions to omniscience, and when these are completely abandoned he advances to the tenth ground.

At the very end of the tenth ground, the Bodhisattva enters a meditative equipoise on emptiness called the 'vajra-like concentration of the path of meditation', which acts as the direct antidote to the very subtle obstructions to omniscience. This concentration is also known as the 'exalted wisdom of the final continuum' because it is the last mind of a limited being. In the next moment he or she has abandoned the very subtle obstructions to omniscience and very subtle dualistic appearances, and has attained the Mahayana Path of No More Learning and become a Conqueror Buddha.

It is impossible to describe all the good qualities of a Buddha. A Buddha's compassion, wisdom, and power are completely beyond conception. With nothing left to obscure his mind, he sees all phenomena throughout the universe as clearly as he sees a jewel held in the palm of his hand. Through the force of his compassion, a Buddha spontaneously does whatever is appropriate to benefit others. He has no need to think about what is the best way to help living beings – he naturally and effortlessly acts in the most beneficial way. Just as the sun does not need to motivate itself to radiate light and heat but does so simply because light and heat are its very nature, so a Buddha does not need to motivate himself to benefit others but does so simply because being beneficial is his very nature.

Like the reflections of the moon that effortlessly appear in any body of still water, a Buddha's emanations spontaneously appear wherever living beings' minds are capable of perceiving them. Buddhas can emanate in any form whatsoever to help living beings. Sometimes they manifest as Buddhists and sometimes as non-Buddhists. They can manifest as women or men, monarchs or tramps, law-abiding citizens or criminals. They can even manifest as animals, as wind or rain, or as mountains or islands. Unless we are a Buddha ourself we cannot possibly say who or what is an emanation of a Buddha.

Of all the ways in which a Buddha helps living beings, the supreme way is by emanating as a Spiritual Guide. Through his or her teachings and immaculate example, an authentic Spiritual Guide leads his or her disciples along the spiritual path to liberation and enlightenment. If we meet a qualified Mahayana Spiritual Guide and put into practice everything he or she teaches, we will definitely attain full enlightenment and become a Conqueror Buddha. We will then be in a position to repay the kindness of all living beings by liberating them from the sufferings of samsara and leading them to the supreme bliss of Buddhahood.

Dedication

I have written this book, *Introduction to Buddhism*, with a pure motivation. Through the virtue I have collected by composing this book, and through all the other virtues of myself and others, may pure Buddhadharma flourish throughout this world. May all mother beings be released from the prison of samsara as quickly as possible, and may they attain the supreme happiness of a Conqueror Buddha.

Geshe Kelsang Gyatso
Manjushri Mahayana
Buddhist Centre

Buddha's Enlightenment Day
June 1992

Appendix I

THE COMMITMENTS OF GOING FOR REFUGE

When we go for refuge we undertake to observe twelve special commitments. By observing these sincerely we protect our mind of refuge, and it gradually becomes more powerful. These commitments lay the foundation for all the realizations of the stages of the path. Realizing this we should not regard them as a burden, but practise them joyfully and sincerely.

Within the twelve commitments there are six specific commitments and six general commitments. The six specific commitments are so called because they are related specifically to each of the Three Jewels. There are two commitments related to Buddha, two related to Dharma, and two related to Sangha. In each case there is one thing to abandon and one thing to practise. The remaining six commitments apply equally to Buddha, Dharma, and Sangha. These twelve commitments will now be briefly explained.

THE TWO COMMITMENTS SPECIFICALLY
RELATED TO BUDDHA

1 Not to go for refuge to teachers who contradict Buddha's view, or to samsaric gods. By going for refuge to Buddha we have a commitment to abandon going for ultimate refuge to teachers who contradict Buddha's view, or to worldly gods. This does not mean that we cannot receive help from others; it means that we do not rely upon others to provide ultimate protection from suffering.

2 To regard any image of Buddha as an actual Buddha. By going for refuge to Buddha we also have a commitment to regard any image of Buddha as an actual Buddha. Whenever we see a statue of Buddha, whether it is made of gold or anything else, we should see it as an actual Buddha. We should disregard the material or the quality of the craftsmanship, and pay homage by making offerings and prostrations, and by going for refuge. If we practise like this our merit will increase abundantly.

THE TWO COMMITMENTS SPECIFICALLY RELATED TO DHARMA

3 Not to harm others. By going for refuge to Dharma we have a commitment to abandon harming others. Instead of treating others badly we should try, with the best motivation, to benefit them whenever we can. We first need to concentrate on reducing harmful thoughts and generating a beneficial intention towards those who are close to us, such as our friends and family. When we have developed a good heart towards these people we can gradually extend our practice to include more and more people, until finally we have a good heart towards all living beings. If we can abandon harmful thoughts and always have a beneficial intention, we will easily attain the realizations of great love and great compassion. In this way we begin to increase our compassion, which is the very essence of Buddhadharma, from the very beginning of our practice of going for refuge.

4 To regard all Dharma scriptures as the actual Dharma Jewel. By going for refuge to Dharma we also have a commitment to regard all Dharma scriptures as the actual Dharma Jewel. Dharma is the source of all health and happiness. Since we cannot see actual Dharma Jewels with our eyes, we need to regard Dharma texts as actual Dharma Jewels. Actual Dharma Jewels arise only as a result of learning, contemplating, and meditating on the meaning of the scriptures. We need to respect every letter of the scriptures, and every letter of explanation of Buddha's teaching. Therefore, we must treat Dharma books with great care and avoid walking over them or putting them in inappropriate places where they might be damaged or misused. Each time we neglect or spoil our Dharma books we create the cause to become more ignorant because these actions are similar to the action of abandoning Dharma. Once the great Tibetan Teacher Geshe Sharawa saw some people playing carelessly with their Dharma books and he said to them 'You should not do that. You already have enough ignorance. Why do you want to make yourselves even more ignorant?'

THE TWO COMMITMENTS SPECIFICALLY
RELATED TO SANGHA

5 Not to allow ourself to be influenced by people who reject Buddha's teaching. By going for refuge to the Sangha we have a commitment to stop being influenced by people who reject Buddha's teaching. This does not mean that we should abandon these people, merely that we should not let their views influence our mind. Without abandoning love and consideration for others, we need to be vigilant and make sure that we are not being led astray by their bad habits and unsound advice.

6 To regard anyone who wears the robes of an ordained person as an actual Sangha Jewel. By going for refuge to the Sangha we also have a commitment to acknowledge anyone who wears the robes of an ordained person as an actual Sangha Jewel. Even if ordained Sangha are poor, we still need to pay respect to them because they are keeping moral discipline, and this is something very rare and precious.

THE SIX GENERAL COMMITMENTS

7 To go for refuge to the Three Jewels again and again, remembering their good qualities and the differences between them. Dharma is like a boat that can carry us across the ocean of samsara, Buddha is like the skilful navigator of the boat, and the Sangha are like the crew. Remembering this, we should go for refuge again and again to the Three Jewels.

8 To offer the first portion of whatever we eat and drink to the Three Jewels, while remembering their kindness. Since we need to eat and drink several times each day, if we always offer the first portion of our food or drink to the Three Jewels remembering their kindness, we will greatly increase our merit. We can do this with the following prayer:

> I make this offering to you, Buddha Shakyamuni,
> Whose mind is the synthesis of all Buddha Jewels,
> Whose speech is the synthesis of all Dharma Jewels,
> Whose body is the synthesis of all Sangha Jewels.
> O Blessed One, please accept this and bless my
> mind.

> OM AH HUM   (3x)

It is important always to remember Buddha's kindness. All our happiness is a result of Buddha's kindness because all Buddha's actions are pervaded by compassion and concern for others, and it is these actions that enable us to perform virtuous actions that are the cause of our happiness.

Without Buddha's kindness we would not know the real causes of happiness, or the real causes of suffering. Buddha taught us how all happiness and suffering depend upon the mind. He showed us how to abandon those states of mind that cause suffering and cultivate those states of mind that cause happiness. In other words, he taught us perfect methods for overcoming suffering and attaining happiness. No one else taught us these methods. How kind Buddha is!

Our own human body is proof of Buddha's kindness. It is by virtue of Buddha's blessings and instructions that we were able to create the cause to take rebirth in a human form, with all the freedoms and endowments necessary for spiritual practice. If we are now able to learn Dharma and meet Spiritual Guides, it is only through Buddha's kindness. We can now practise the methods that lead to full enlightenment and gain spiritual realizations only because Buddha was kind enough to turn the Wheel of Dharma and show his example in this world. Even the small wisdom we possess to discriminate between what is beneficial and what is harmful, and to identify Buddha's teaching as worthwhile, is a result of Buddha's kindness.

We should not think that Buddha helps only those who follow him. Buddha attained enlightenment to benefit all living beings. He manifests in many different forms, sometimes even as non-Buddhist teachers, to help others. There is no sentient being who has not benefited from the kindness of Buddha.

9 With compassion, always to encourage others to go for refuge. We should always try to help others to go for refuge, but we should do so skilfully. If we know someone who is interested in Dharma we should help them to develop the causes of going for refuge: fear of suffering and faith in the Three Jewels. We can talk to them about impermanence – how the conditions of this life change and how our body will grow old and decay – and we can talk about the sufferings of ageing, sickness, and death. We can talk about what will happen after death, about the different types of rebirth, and about how all types of rebirth are in the nature of suffering. If we skilfully introduce these things into our conversations, the other person will begin to lose his complacency and, when he starts to feel uneasy, he will naturally want to find out what can be done. At this point we can explain about Buddha, Dharma, and Sangha, and how they can help us. Then we can explain how to go for refuge.

If we help someone else tactfully in this way, without being arrogant or impatient, we will bring them real benefit. It is never certain that the material gifts we give to others will actually help them; sometimes they even cause more problems. The best way to help others is to lead them into Dharma. If we cannot give elaborate explanations, we can at least give proper advice to those who are unhappy and help them to solve their problems by means of Dharma.

10 To go for refuge at least three times during the day and three times during night, remembering the benefits of going for refuge. So that we never forget the Three Jewels we should go for refuge once every four hours, or at least three times during the day and three times during the night. If we never forget the Three Jewels and regularly contemplate the benefits of going for refuge, we will gain realizations very quickly. We should be like a businessman who never forgets his projects even while he is relaxing.

11 To perform every action with complete trust in the Three Jewels. We should rely upon the Three Jewels in everything that we do. In this way all our actions will be successful. There is no need to seek the inspiration and blessings of worldly gods, but we should always try to receive the blessings of Buddha, Dharma, and Sangha by making offerings and requests.

12 Never to forsake the Three Jewels, even at the cost of our life, or as a joke. We should never abandon the Three Jewels because going for refuge is the foundation of all Dharma realizations. Once a Buddhist was taken captive and his enemy said to him 'Give up your refuge in Buddha or I shall kill you.' He refused to forsake his refuge and was killed, but when clairvoyants looked they saw that he had immediately been reborn as a god.

Appendix II

THE MAHAYANA SUTRA OF THE THREE SUPERIOR HEAPS

Namo: The Bodhisattva's Confession of Moral Downfalls

I, whose name is . . . , at all times go for refuge to the Guru, go for refuge to the Buddha, go for refuge to the Dharma, go for refuge to the Sangha.

To the Teacher, Blessed One, Tathagata, Foe Destroyer, Completely Perfect Buddha, Glorious Conqueror Shakyamuni I prostrate.

To the Tathagata Complete Subduer with the Essence of Vajra I prostrate.

To the Tathagata Jewel of Radiant Light I prostrate.

To the Tathagata Powerful King of the Nagas I prostrate.

To the Tathagata Leader of the Heroes I prostrate.

To the Tathagata Glorious Pleasure I prostrate.

To the Tathagata Jewel Fire I prostrate.

To the Tathagata Jewel Moonlight I prostrate.

To the Tathagata Meaningful to Behold I prostrate.

To the Tathagata Jewel Moon I prostrate.

To the Tathagata Stainless One I prostrate.

To the Tathagata Bestower of Glory I prostrate.

To the Tathagata Pure One I prostrate.

To the Tathagata Transforming with Purity I prostrate.

To the Tathagata Water Deity I prostrate.

To the Tathagata God of Water Deities I prostrate.

To the Tathagata Glorious Excellence I prostrate.

To the Tathagata Glorious Sandalwood I prostrate.

To the Tathagata Endless Splendour I prostrate.

To the Tathagata Glorious Light I prostrate.

To the Tathagata Glorious One without Sorrow
I prostrate.

To the Tathagata Son without Craving I prostrate.

To the Tathagata Glorious Flower I prostrate.

To the Tathagata Clearly Knowing through Enjoying
Pure Radiance I prostrate.

To the Tathagata Clearly Knowing through Enjoying
Lotus Radiance I prostrate.

To the Tathagata Glorious Wealth I prostrate.

To the Tathagata Glorious Mindfulness I prostrate.

To the Tathagata Glorious Name of Great Renown
I prostrate.

To the Tathagata King of the Victory Banner Head of
the Powerful Ones I prostrate.

To the Tathagata Glorious One Complete Subduer
I prostrate.

To the Tathagata Great Victor in Battle I prostrate.

To the Tathagata Glorious One Complete Subduer
Passed Beyond I prostrate.

To the Tathagata Glorious Array Illuminating All
   I prostrate.

To the Tathagata Jewel Lotus Great Subduer I prostrate.

To the Tathagata Foe Destroyer, Completely Perfect
   Buddha, King of Mount Meru Seated Firmly on a
   Jewel and a Lotus I prostrate.

O all you [Tathagatas] and all the others, however many
Tathagatas, the Foe Destroyers, the Completely Perfect
Buddhas, the Blessed Ones there are dwelling and abid-
ing in all the worldly realms of the ten directions, all you
Buddhas, the Blessed Ones, please listen to me.

In this life and in all my lives since beginningless time,
in all my places of rebirth whilst wandering in samsara,
I have done negative actions, have ordered them to be
done, and have rejoiced in their being done. I have stolen
the property of the bases of offering, the property of the
Sangha, and the property of the Sanghas of the ten directions, have ordered it to be stolen, and have rejoiced in
it being stolen. I have committed the five unbounded
heinous actions, have ordered them to be committed, and
have rejoiced in their being committed. I have completely
engaged in the paths of the ten non-virtuous actions, have
ordered others to engage in them, and have rejoiced in
their engaging in them.

Being obstructed by such karmic obstructions, I shall
become a hell being, or I shall be born as an animal, or I
shall go to the land of the hungry ghosts, or I shall be
born as a barbarian in an irreligious country, or I shall be
born as a long-life god, or I shall come to have incomplete
senses, or I shall come to hold wrong views, or I shall
have no opportunity to please a Buddha.

All such karmic obstructions I declare in the presence
of the Buddhas, the Blessed Ones, who have become
exalted wisdom, who have become 'eyes', who have
become witnesses, who have become valid, who see with

their wisdom. I confess without concealing or hiding any-thing, and from now on I shall avoid and refrain from such actions.

All you Buddhas, the Blessed Ones, please listen to me. In this life and in all my previous lives since beginning-less time, in all my places of rebirth whilst wandering in samsara, whatever root of virtue there is in my giving to others, even in my giving a morsel of food to one born as an animal; whatever root of virtue there is in my main-taining moral discipline; whatever root of virtue there is in my actions conducive to great liberation; whatever root of virtue there is in my acting to fully ripen sentient beings; whatever root of virtue there is in my generating a supreme mind of enlightenment; and whatever root of virtue there is in my unsurpassed exalted wisdom; all of these assembled, gathered, and collected together, by fully dedicating them to the unsurpassed, to that of which there is no higher, to that which is even higher than the high, and to that which surpasses the unsur-passed, I fully dedicate to the unsurpassed, perfect, complete enlightenment.

Just as the Buddhas, the Blessed Ones of the past, have dedicated fully, just as the Buddhas, the Blessed Ones who are yet to come, will dedicate fully, and just as the Buddhas, the Blessed Ones who are living now, dedicate fully, so too do I dedicate fully.

I confess individually all negative actions. I rejoice in all merit. I beseech and request all the Buddhas. May I attain the holy, supreme, unsurpassed, exalted wisdom.

Whoever are the Conquerors, the supreme beings living now, those of the past, and likewise those who are yet to come, with a boundless ocean of praise for all your good qualities, and with my palms pressed together I go close to you for refuge.

This concludes the Mahayana Sutra entitled the *Sutra of the Three Superior Heaps*.

Glossary

Alertness A mental factor that is a type of wisdom that examines our activity of body, speech, and mind and knows whether or not faults are developing.

Aspiring bodhichitta A bodhichitta that is a mere wish to attain enlightenment for the benefit of all sentient beings.

Attachment A deluded mental factor that observes a contaminated object, regards it as a cause of happiness, and wishes for it. See *Joyful Path* and *Understanding the Mind*.

Bardo See *Intermediate state.*

Blessing 'Jin gyi lab' in Tibetan. The transformation of our mind from a negative state to a positive state, from an unhappy state to a happy state, or from a state of weakness to a state of strength through the inspiration of holy beings such as our Spiritual Guide, the Buddhas, and Bodhisattvas.

Bodhichitta Sanskrit word for 'mind of enlightenment'. 'Bodhi' means enlightenment and 'chitta' means mind. There are two types of bodhichitta: conventional bodhichitta and ultimate bodhichitta. Generally speaking, the term 'bodhichitta' refers to conventional bodhichitta, which is a primary mind motivated by great compassion that spontaneously seeks enlightenment to benefit all sentient beings. Conventional bodhichitta is of two types: aspiring bodhichitta and engaging bodhichitta. Ultimate bodhichitta is a wisdom motivated by conventional bodhichitta that directly realizes emptiness, the ultimate nature of phenomena. See also *Aspiring bodhichitta* and *Engaging bodhichitta*. See *Joyful Path, Meaningful to Behold*, and *Universal Compassion*.

Bodhisattva A person who has generated spontaneous bodhichitta but who has not yet become a Buddha. From the moment a practitioner generates a non-artificial, or spontaneous, bodhichitta he or she becomes a Bodhisattva and enters the first Mahayana path, the path of accumulation. An ordinary Bodhisattva is one who has not realized emptiness directly, and a Superior Bodhisattva is one who has attained a direct realization of emptiness. See *Joyful Path* and *Meaningful to Behold*.

Brahma A worldly god.

Buddha A being who has completely abandoned all delusions and their imprints. There are many beings who have become Buddhas in the past, and there are many who will become Buddhas in the future. See *Joyful Path*.

Buddha nature The root mind of a sentient being, and its ultimate nature. Buddha nature, Buddha lineage, and Buddha seed are synonymous. All sentient beings have Buddha nature and therefore have the potential to attain Buddhahood.

Buddha's bodies A Buddha has four bodies – the Wisdom Truth Body, the Nature Body, the Enjoyment Body, and the Emanation Bodies. The first is Buddha's omniscient mind; the second is the emptiness, or ultimate nature, of his mind; the third is his actual Form Body, which is very subtle; and the fourth, of which each Buddha manifests a countless number, are gross Form Bodies that are visible to ordinary beings. The Wisdom Truth Body and the Nature Body are both included within the Truth Body, and the Enjoyment Body and the Emanation Bodies are both included within the Form Body. See *Joyful Path* and *Ocean of Nectar*.

Buddhadharma Buddha's teachings and the inner realizations attained by practising them.

Buddha Shakyamuni The fourth of one thousand Buddhas who are to appear in this world during this Fortunate Aeon. The first three were Krakuchchhanda, Kanakamuni, and Kashyapa. The fifth Buddha will be Maitreya.

Central channel The principal channel at the very centre of the body where the channel wheels are located. See *Clear Light of Bliss.*

Chakravatin king An extremely fortunate being who has accumulated a vast amount of merit and as a result has taken rebirth as a king with dominion over all four continents, or at the very least over one of the four continents. At present there are no chakravatin kings in our world, and there is no one who has complete dominion over our continent, Jambudipa. See *Great Treasury of Merit.*

Channel wheel 'Chakra' in Sanskrit. A focal centre where secondary channels branch out from the central channel. Meditating on these points can cause the inner winds to enter the central channel. See *Clear Light of Bliss.*

Chenrezig The embodiment of the compassion of all the Buddhas. At the time of Buddha Shakyamuni he manifested as a Bodhisattva disciple.

Clairvoyance Abilities that arise from special concentration. There are five principal types of clairvoyance: eye clairvoyance (the ability to see subtle and distant forms), ear clairvoyance (the ability to hear subtle and distant sounds), remembering former lives, knowing others' minds, and the clairvoyance of miracle powers (the ability to emanate various forms by mind). Some beings such as bardo beings and some humans and spirits have contaminated clairvoyance that is developed due to karma, but these are not actual clairvoyance.

Clear light A manifest very subtle mind that perceives an appearance like clear, empty space. See *Clear Light of Bliss* and *Great Treasury of Merit.*

Collection of merit A virtuous action motivated by bodhichitta that is a main cause of attaining the Form Body of a Buddha. Examples are: making offerings and prostrations to holy beings with bodhichitta motivation, and the practice of the perfections of giving, moral discipline, and patience. See also *Buddha's bodies.*

Collection of wisdom A virtuous mental action motivated by bodhichitta that is a main cause for attaining the Truth Body of a Buddha. Examples are: listening to, contemplating, and meditating on emptiness with bodhichitta motivation. See also *Buddha's bodies.*

Conceptual mind A thought that apprehends its object through a generic image. See *Understanding the Mind.*

Confession Purification of negative karma by means of the four opponent powers – the power of reliance, the power of regret, the power of the antidote, and the power of promise. See *The Bodhisattva Vow.*

Conscientiousness A mental factor that, in dependence upon effort, cherishes what is virtuous and guards the mind from delusion and non-virtue. See *Joyful Path*, *Meaningful to Behold*, and *Understanding the Mind.*

Conventional nature See *Ultimate nature.*

Degenerate times A period when spiritual activity degenerates.

Delusion A mental factor that arises from inappropriate attention and functions to make the mind unpeaceful and uncontrolled. There are three main delusions: ignorance, attachment, and hatred. From these, all other delusions such as jealousy, pride, and deluded doubt arise. See also *Innate delusions* and *Intellectually-formed delusions*. See *Joyful Path* and *Understanding the Mind.*

Demon 'Mara' in Sanskrit. Anything that obstructs the attainment of liberation or enlightenment. There are four principal types of demon: the demon of the delusions, the demon of the contaminated aggregates, the demon of death, and the Devaputra demons. Of these, only the last are actual sentient beings. The principal Devaputra demon is wrathful Ishvara, the highest of the desire realm gods who inhabits the Land Controlling Others' Emanations. Buddha is called a 'Conqueror' because he has conquered all four types of demon. See *Heart of Wisdom* and *Ocean of Nectar.*

Desire realm The environment of humans, animals, hungry ghosts, hell beings, and the gods who enjoy the five objects of desire.

Dharma See *Buddhadharma.*

Dharma Protectors Manifestations of Buddhas or Bodhisattvas whose main function is to eliminate obstacles and gather all necessary conditions for pure Dharma practitioners. See *Heart Jewel.*

Dharmapala See *Dharma Protectors.*

Dualistic appearance The appearance to mind of an object together with the inherent existence of that object. See *Heart of Wisdom* and *Ocean of Nectar.*

Emptiness Lack of inherent existence, the ultimate nature of all phenomena. See *Heart of Wisdom, Joyful Path,* and *Ocean of Nectar.*

Engaging bodhichitta A bodhichitta held by the Bodhisattva vows.

Enlightenment Usually the full enlightenment of Buddhahood. There are three levels of enlightenment: small enlightenment, or the enlightenment of a Hearer; middling enlightenment, or the enlightenment of a Solitary Conqueror; and great enlightenment, or the enlightenment of a Buddha. An enlightenment is a liberation and a true cessation. See *Clear Light of Bliss, Joyful Path,* and *Ocean of Nectar.*

Foe Destroyer 'Arhat' in Sanskrit. A practitioner who has abandoned all delusions and their seeds by training on the spiritual paths, and who will never again be born in samsara. In this context, the term 'foe' refers to the delusions.

Form realm The environment of the gods who possess form.

Formless realm The environment of the gods who do not possess form.

Four noble truths True sufferings, true origins, true cessations, and true paths. They are called 'noble' truths because they are supreme objects of meditation. Through meditation on these four objects we can realize ultimate truth directly and thus become a noble, or Superior, being. Sometimes referred to as the 'Four truths of Superiors'. See *Heart of Wisdom* and *Joyful Path*.

Generic image The appearing object of a conceptual mind. See *Heart of Wisdom* and *Understanding the Mind*.

Geshe A title given by the Kadampa Monasteries to accomplished Buddhist scholars.

Geshe Langri Tangpa (AD 1054-1123) A great Kadampa Geshe who was famous for his realization of exchanging self with others. He composed *Eight Verses of Training the Mind*.

Great liberation Great enlightenment, or Buddhahood.

Ground Any realization maintained by a spontaneous realization of renunciation or bodhichitta. In general, ground and path are synonyms. The ten grounds are the realizations of Superior Bodhisattvas. They are: Very Joyful, Stainless, Luminous, Radiant, Difficult to Overcome, Approaching, Gone Afar, Immovable, Good Intelligence, and Cloud of Dharma. See *Ocean of Nectar*.

Imprint There are two types of imprint: imprints of actions and imprints of delusions. Every action leaves an imprint on the mind. These imprints are karmic potentialities to experience certain effects in the future. The imprints of delusions remain even after the delusions themselves have been abandoned. Imprints of delusions are obstructions to omniscience. They are completely abandoned only by Buddhas.

Indra A worldly god. See *Heart of Wisdom*.

Innate delusions Delusions that are not the product of intellectual speculation, but arise naturally. See *Joyful Path* and *Understanding the Mind*.

Inner winds Special winds related to the mind that flow through the channels of our body. Our mind cannot function without these winds. See *Clear Light of Bliss* and *Great Treasury of Merit*.

Intellectually-formed delusions Delusions that arise as a result of relying upon incorrect reasoning or mistaken tenets. See *Joyful Path* and *Understanding the Mind*.

Intention A mental factor that functions to move its primary mind to its object. It functions to engage the mind in virtuous, non-virtuous, and neutral objects. All bodily and verbal actions are initiated by the mental factor intention. See *Joyful Path* and *Understanding the Mind*.

Intermediate state 'Bardo' in Tibetan. The state between death and rebirth. It begins the moment the consciousness leaves the body and ceases the moment the consciousness enters the body of the next life. See *Joyful Path*.

Je Tsongkhapa (AD 1357-1419) An emanation of the Wisdom Buddha Manjushri whose appearance in fourteenth-century Tibet as a monk was predicted by Buddha. He restored the purity of Buddha's doctrine and demonstrated how to practise pure Dharma during degenerate times. His tradition later became known as the 'Ganden Tradition'. See *Heart Jewel* and *Great Treasury of Merit*.

Kadampa A follower of the Kadampa Tradition passed down from Atisha and his disciple Dromtönpa. Up to the time of Je Tsongkhapa the tradition is known as the 'Old Kadampa Tradition' and after the time of Je Tsongkhapa it is known as the 'New Kadampa Tradition'.

Mantra Literally, 'mind protection'. Mantra protects the mind from ordinary appearances and conceptions. See *Heart of Wisdom* and *Guide to Dakini Land*.

Mara See *Demon*.

Meditative equipoise Single-pointed concentration on a virtuous object such as emptiness.

Mental awareness An awareness that is developed in dependence upon its uncommon dominant condition, a mental power. See *Understanding the Mind*.

Mental suppleness A flexibility of mind induced by virtuous concentration. See *Clear Light of Bliss*, *Joyful Path*, and *Understanding the Mind*.

Mindfulness A mental factor that functions not to forget the object realized by the primary mind. See *Clear Light of Bliss*, *Joyful Path*, *Meaningful to Behold*, and *Understanding the Mind*.

Miracle powers See *Clairvoyance*.

Nine mental abidings Nine levels of concentration leading to tranquil abiding. They are: placing the mind, continual placement, replacement, close placement, controlling, pacifying, completely pacifying, single-pointedness, and placement in equipoise. See *Meaningful to Behold*, *Joyful Path*, and *Clear Light of Bliss*.

Non-conceptual mind A cognizer to which its object appears clearly without being mixed with a generic image. See *Understanding the Mind*.

Object of negation An object explicitly negated by a mind realizing a negative phenomenon.

Path See *Ground*.

Puja A ceremony in which offerings and other acts of devotion are performed in front of holy beings.

Pure Land A pure environment in which there are no true sufferings. There are many Pure Lands. For example, Tushita is the Pure Land of Buddha Maitreya, Sukhavati is the Pure Land of Buddha Amitabha, and Dakini Land, or Keajra, is the Pure Land of Buddha Vajrayogini. See *Guide to Dakini Land* and *Heart Jewel*.

Sangha According to the Vinaya tradition, any community of four or more fully ordained monks. In general, ordained or lay people who take Bodhisattva vows or Tantric vows can also be said to be Sangha.

Secret Mantra Synonymous with Tantra. Secret Mantra teachings are distinguished from Sutra teachings in that they reveal methods for training the mind by bringing the future result, or Buddhahood, into the present path. Secret Mantra is the supreme path to full enlightenment. The term 'mantra' indicates that it is Buddha's special instruction for protecting our mind from ordinary appearances and conceptions. Practitioners of Secret Mantra overcome ordinary appearances and conceptions by visualizing their body, environment, enjoyments, and deeds as those of a Buddha. The term 'secret' indicates that the practices are to be done in private, and that they can be practised only by those who have received a Tantric empowerment. See *Great Treasury of Merit*, *Guide to Dakini Land*, and *Clear Light of Bliss*.

Self-cherishing A mental attitude that considers oneself to be precious or important. It is regarded as a principal object to be abandoned by Bodhisattvas. See *Universal Compassion*, *Joyful Path*, and *Meaningful to Behold*.

Self-grasping A conceptual mind that holds any phenomenon to be inherently existent. The mind of self-grasping gives rise to all other delusions such as anger and attachment. It is the root cause of all suffering and dissatisfaction. See *Joyful Path*, *Heart of Wisdom*, and *Ocean of Nectar*.

Sense awareness An awareness that is developed in dependence upon its uncommon dominant condition, a sense power possessing form. See *Understanding the Mind*.

Shantideva (AD 687–763) A great Indian Buddhist scholar and meditation master. He composed *Guide to the Bodhisattva's Way of Life*. See *Meaningful to Behold*.

Spiritual Guide Any Teacher who guides us along the Spiritual Path. See *Joyful Path*, *Great Treasury of Merit*, and *Heart Jewel*.

Superior being 'Arya' in Sanskrit. A being who has a direct realization of emptiness. There are Hinayana Superiors and Mahayana Superiors.

Superior seeing A special wisdom that sees its object clearly and that is maintained by tranquil abiding and the special suppleness that is induced by investigation. See *Joyful Path*.

Suppleness See *Mental suppleness.*

Supreme Emanation Body A special Emanation Body displaying the thirty-two major signs and eighty minor indications that can be seen by ordinary beings only if they have very pure karma. See also *Buddha's bodies.*

Sutra The teachings of Buddha that are open to everyone to practise. These include Buddha's teachings of the three Turnings of the Wheel of Dharma.

Tantra See *Secret Mantra.*

Three Jewels The three objects of refuge: Buddha Jewel, Dharma Jewel, and Sangha Jewel. They are called 'Jewels' because they are both rare and precious. See *Joyful Path.*

Tranquil abiding A concentration that possesses the special bliss of suppleness of body and mind that is attained in dependence upon completing the nine mental abidings. See *Clear Light of Bliss, Joyful Path,* and *Meaningful to Behold.*

Transference of consciousness A practice for transferring the consciousness to a Pure Land at the time of death. See *Great Treasury of Merit.*

Ultimate nature All phenomena have two natures – a conventional nature and an ultimate nature. A table, for example, and its shape, colour, and so forth are all the conventional nature of the table; and the table's lack of inherent existence is its ultimate nature. The conventional nature of a phenomenon is a conventional truth and its ultimate nature is an ultimate truth. See *Heart of Wisdom* and *Heart Jewel.*

Vajra-like concentration The last moment of the Mahayana path of meditation. It is the antidote to the very subtle obstructions to omniscience. In the next moment one attains the Mahayana Path of No More Learning, or Buddhahood.

Further Reading

If you have enjoyed reading this book and would like to find out more about Buddhist thought and practice, here are some other books by Geshe Kelsang Gyatso that you might like to read:

Joyful Path of Good Fortune

- One of the clearest explanations of the entire Buddhist path to enlightenment available in the West
- Reveals practical methods for transforming our mind with meditation, to attain peace and happiness for ourself and others
- Enables us to appreciate the essential meaning of all Buddha's teachings and to apply them in our daily life

Universal Compassion

- An excellent introduction to the Mahayana Buddhist teachings on training the mind
- Provides step-by-step instructions on how to develop an authentic mind of universal compassion, the resolve to free all living beings from suffering
- Explains in detail how we can turn all life situations – even the most difficult – into opportunities for personal development

A Meditation Handbook

- Step-by-step meditation manual for beginners and advanced meditators alike
- Provides a clear and practical explanation of what meditation is and how it works

- Presents twenty-one different Buddhist meditations which together constitute the entire path to enlightenment, and which we can practise individually or as a cycle

Meaningful to Behold

- The first entire commentary in English to the great Indian classic, *Guide to the Bodhisattva's Way of Life* by Shantideva
- Highly acclaimed presentation of a completely pure, wise, and compassionate lifestyle
- Practical advice on how we can develop and maintain authentic compassion for others, and engage in the actual practices that lead to full enlightenment

Heart of Wisdom

- A commentary to the *Heart Sutra*, one of the most popular and well-known of Mahayana Buddhist scriptures
- Provides a lucid explanation of emptiness, the ultimate nature of reality
- Shows how we can gain an initial understanding of emptiness, and how we can use this understanding to overcome obstacles to both temporary and ultimate happiness

All these books are available from Tharpa Publications, Kilnwick Percy Hall, Pocklington, York YO4 2UF, or from a bookshop in your area.

If you would like to attend study and meditation courses based on Geshe Kelsang's books, please ask for details of your nearest New Kadampa Tradition Centre. A list of Centres is available from:

James Belither
Secretary
New Kadampa Tradition (NKT)
Conishead Priory
Ulverston
Cumbria, LA12 9QQ, UK
Tel 0229-584029

Index

145